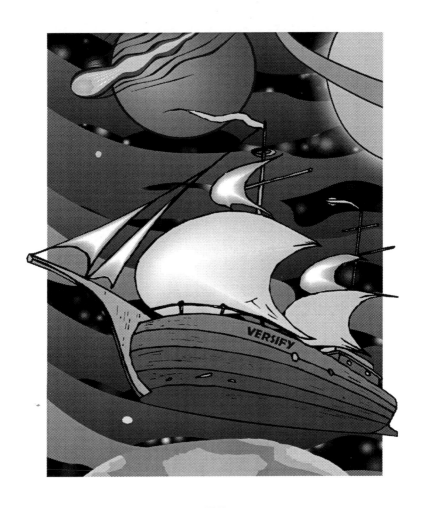

POETIC VOYAGES
SOUTH OXFORDSHIRE

Edited by Simon Harwin

First published in Great Britain in 2002 by
YOUNG WRITERS
Remus House,
Coltsfoot Drive,
Peterborough, PE2 9JX
Telephone (01733) 890066

All Rights Reserved

Copyright Contributors 2001

HB ISBN 0 75433 480 5
SB ISBN 0 75433 481 3

FOREWORD

Young Writers was established in 1991 with the aim to promote creative writing in children, to make reading and writing poetry fun.

This year once again, proved to be a tremendous success with over 88,000 entries received nationwide.

The Poetic Voyages competition has shown us the high standard of work and effort that children are capable of today. It is a reflection of the teaching skills in schools, the enthusiasm and creativity they have injected into their pupils shines clearly within this anthology.

The task of selecting poems was therefore a difficult one but nevertheless, an enjoyable experience. We hope you are as pleased with the final selection in *Poetic Voyages South Oxfordshire* as we are.

CONTENTS

Carswell Primary School
Evan Key	1
Lottie Buttar	1
Sasha Muddiman	2
Josh Brooks	2
Louise Mortimer	3
Jessica Robinson	3
Lisa Roberts	4
Steven Dann	4
Nicholas Williams	5
Jess Burton	5
Harry McCarthy	6
Natasha Cattemull	6
Alice Samways	7
Charleen Meredith	7
Elisha Fiddaman	8
Brittany Chandler	8
Daniella Rogers	9
Lauren Brant	10
Gemma Harling	10

Clifton Hampden CE Primary School
James Bell	11
Camilla Farrant	11
Catherine Curran	12
Elisha Riel	12
Terri Ann Greenaway	13
Melanie Farmer	14
Alex Wood	14

Crowmarsh Gifford CE Primary School
Josh Selwood	15
Henry Fletcher	15
Samuel Diserens	15
Barnaby Sayce	16
Naomi Bosworth	16

Thomas Reed	16
Louise Bodeker	17
Ceinor Sadler	17

Fir Tree Junior School

Stephanie Cummings	18
Tyrone Chainey	19
Emma Chapman	20
Thomas Saunders	21
Mickey Woods	22
Leanne Palmer	24
Lisa Nicholls	26
Jake Clarke	28
Kieran Bowen	30
Emma Mundy	32
Jennifer Graham	34
Luke Wood	36
Francesca McGuinness	38
Charlotte Douglas-Gilbert	40
Sarah Morris	42
Jonathan Smith	43
Keeley Green	44
Robbie Grant	46
Chrissie Atkins	47
Paris Sandiford	48
Verity Graham	49
Nicholas Field	50
Demi Reid	52
Liam Johnson	54
Jake Brown	56

Marcham CE Primary School

James Logan	57
Chris Tolley	57
Rachael Dredge	58
Jos Rowe	58
Hannah Fathers	59
Elizabeth Bell	59

Madeleine Dyer	60
Sebastian Crowley	60
Charlie Newman	61
Ashley Richardson	61
Fred Gardner	62
Lauren Gardner	62
Stacey Greenough	62
Rebecca Marsh	63
Alex Turney	63
Sophie Hopgood	63
Sarah Narramore	64
Scott Walker	65
Emily Upjohn	65
Ross Walker	65
Ellen Walton	66
Matthew Ward	66
Gemma Cade	67
Sarah Waterhouse	67
Alicia Simmons	68

Moulsford Preparatory School

Richard Collinson	68
James Newman	69
Leigh Anderson	70
James Ralphs	70
Rory Van Zwanenberg	71
William Greenslade	72
Charlie Macdonald	72
William Emmett	73
Sam Fletcher	74
Gus Bartholomew	74
Joshua Chew	75
Dominic Rothbarth	76
Jack Barker	76
Chris Watts	77
Joe Jones	77

Rupert House School

Alexandra Hopkinson	78
Emma Gibbs	78
Emily Granger	79
Alexandra Boardman	79
Jennifer Taylor	80
Alexandra Barbour	81
Eleanor Hollier	82
Emma Collinson	82
Emily Shawcross	83
Charly Halsall	84
Davina Collas	84
Sarah Richards	85
Louisa Baczor	85
Jessica Mace	86
Larissa Batt	86
Victoria Williams-Gray	87
Annie Elphick	87
Katherine Innes	88
Kate Swann	88
Charlotte Martin	89
Tabitha Juster	90
Melissa King	90
Jessica Moran	91
Sophie Rothbarth	91
Alicia Holder	92
Daisy Lea	92
Charly Binney	93
Lucy Mace	93
Alice Thornton	94
Elizabeth Sanders	94
Jessica Waddington	95
Stephanie Rigby	96

St Andrews School, Wantage

Tabitha Jenkins	96
Rachel Spooner	97
Charlie Instone	97

Michael Garner	98
Georgia Phetmanh	98
Jessica Murray	99
Ellie Wood	100
Nicholas Wood	100
Rebecca White	101
Elizabeth Vickers	101
Clare Gent	102
Arabella Day	102
James Ballantyne	103
Toby Silverstone	104
Serena Boheimer	104
Olivia Palmer	105
Kate Instone	106
Eloise Jenkins	106
Alex Ballantyne	107
Vicki Coxon	107
Thomas Smith	108
Thomas Masson	108
Hannah Watts	109
Charlotte Lewis-Pryde	110
Hannah Stevenson	110

St Edmund's RC Primary School, Abingdon

Charlotte Drew	111
Aislinn Baird	111
Hannah Brown	112
John Galvin	112
Sophie Bennett	113
Jack Dingwall	113
Jessica FitzGerald	114
Laura Molloy	114
Michaela Barklie	115
Emily Pepperell	115
Aislinn Campbell	116
Samantha Crossan	117
Stephanie Bennett	118
Charlotte Irwin	118

Georgina St John	119
Kayleigh Pratt	119
Kimberley Daly	120
Ruben Everett	121

St Mary's School, Henley-on-Thames

Emily Tooher	121
Purdey Miles	122
James Burke & Krysha Shahi	122
Amy Biart & Matthew Welfare	123
Christopher Jeanes & Hannah Dodds	123
Celeste Harber & Elliott Butler	124
Emily Atkinson	124
Lauren Fisher	125
Isobel Dodds	125
Alex Barker	126

Uffington Primary School

Emily Jones	126
J J Keene	127
Andrew Baxter	127
James Allen	128
Peter Jones	128
Mark Hagreen	129
Peter Long	129
Chris Keene	130
Ollie Baily & Angus de Wilton	131
Matthew Young	131
Jason Haynes	132
Tom de Wilton	133
Peter Wren	134
Alex Gaffka	134
Peter Osmond	135

The Poems

ONE OLD ODD ORANGE OCTOPUS

One old odd orange octopus
Two tiny tigers' tails tickle talking tortoise
Three tiny toddlers' toes
Four fine foxes fiddling
Five famous fish flying
Six slithering snakes saving Samuel
Seven soggy socks
Eight enormous elephants estimating eggs
Nine nippy nosey noses
Ten terrible teachers talking together.

Evan Key (7)
Carswell Primary School

ONE OLD ODD OWL

One old odd owl
Two tweeting trolls trotting to Toptown
Three toes taunting twinkling to Tadbury
Four fighting fiddles fiddling for food
Five fierce fingers falling
Six sizzling sliding sticky sausages
Seven slithering sweet snakes sighing
Eight enormous elderly elephants eating eagles' eggs
Nine nightingales noisily nibbling
Ten tiny tickling things.

Lottie Buttar (7)
Carswell Primary School

ONE OLD ODD OCTOPUS

One old odd octopus
Two tiny twinkling tigers talking together
Three tiny teachers talking terribly together
Four fish fiddling fish fingers
Five fighting rats
Six slimy slippery snakes
Seven slow slimy slugs
Eight enormous elephants eating eggs
Nine naughty nails nibbling noses
Ten teachers terrifying tigers.

Sasha Muddiman (7)
Carswell Primary School

ONE OLD OCTOPUS

One old octopus
Two tigers talking
Three talking toddlers
    Four fiddling foxes
Five fiddling fingers
Six sticky singers
Seven sparkling stars
Eight evil elephants
Nine noisy knitters
Ten tiny toes.

Josh Brooks (8)
Carswell Primary School

ONE OLD ODD OPENED ORANGE

One old odd opened orange
Two twizling twisters turning through trees
Three tiny teachers talking terribly
Four fishes fishing
Five fat foxes finding food
Six smelly socks sticking
Seven silver snakes sizzling
Eight enormous elephants eating eggs
Nine naughty newts
Ten terrible tigers talking.

Louise Mortimer (9)
Carswell Primary School

ONE OLD ODD OCTOPUS

One old odd octopus
Two tiny tingly toes talking together
Three terrible teachers tearing tortoises
Four fitting fish fizzling famously
Five fat freezing foxes
Six sizzling sausages
Seven slimy snakes
Eight English elephants
Nine naughty nits
Ten terrible teachers.

Jessica Robinson (7)
Carswell Primary School

ONE OCTOPUS OF OURS

One octopus of ours
Two twinkling tigers talking together
Three terrible tigers tidying up
Four fine fingers fiddling food
Five fat fish fiddling
Six sausages sizzling
Seven slushy seas
Eight enormous elves eating eggs
Nine nice naps
Ten tickly toes.

Lisa Roberts (7)
Carswell Primary School

ONE OLD ORANGE OSTRICH

One old orange ostrich
Two tiny tiddly tigers trying tins
Three tinkly toes
Four fine foxes finding fish
Five fat famous foxes
Six smelly sausages
Seven shining stars
Eight elephants eating eggs
Nine naughty nuggets
Ten tiny tigers.

Steven Dann (7)
Carswell Primary School

ONE ODD OGRE

One odd ogre opening oranges
Two tiny toddlers tickling teachers

Three tortoises thrashing toads
Four fine foxes finding food

Five fiddling fingers fitting famously
Six sausages sizzling stupidly

Seven silly snakes stealing silver
Eight English elephants eating eleven eggs

Nine neat naughty nightingales
Ten termites tickling tall trees.

Nicholas Williams (8)
Carswell Primary School

ONE OBVIOUS OSTRICH

One odd ostrich opened one orange
Two tangling tigers tickling toes
Three tiny tortoise taking time
Four fat fiddlers' fiddling fingers
Five fish frightened for frosty frogs
Six silver sloppy sausages scratching shops
Seven smelly space socks skating
Eight elephants eating eleven eggs
Nine nippy nodding noses
Ten tinkled toes tossing two throats.

Jess Burton (8)
Carswell Primary School

ONE ONLY OVERALL

One only overall
Two ticklish tremendous toes
Three tidy tiny tights
Four fidgeting fighting finances
Five flying flies finishing food
Six sloppy songbirds singing
Seven sleeping symbols slurping
Eight enormous eggs eating emus
Nine nimble nightingales nudging nincompoops
Ten tingling tinkers twinkling their thumbs.

Harry McCarthy (7)
Carswell Primary School

ONE OOZING ORANGE OSTRICH

One oozing orange ostrich
Two tiny tigers twinkling
Three terrifying toddlers trembling
Four flying fossils fishing
Five fidgeting fish fiddling
Six stalks singing sweetly
Seven selfish snakes slipping skilfully
Eight empty elephants eating eleven eggs
Nine naughty Natashas knitting
Ten toes talking terribly.

Natasha Cattemull (8)
Carswell Primary School

ONE OGGLY OCTOPUS

One oggly octopus on an obstacle race
Two toddling toddlers tooting tricks
Three tigers tickling teddies
Four fat foxes falling fast
Five fine fleas fishing flies
Six stupid snakes sipping soup
Seven smelly snails sliding on slime
Eight enormous elephants eating eagerly
Nine noisy gnats nibbling noodles
Ten tumbling terrapins tweeting terribly
Eleven eager eagles embroidered with evergreens
Twelve twinkling turtles tipping tulip tea
Thirteen thin toasts tracking down ten plates.

Alice Samways (8)
Carswell Primary School

ONE OBVIOUS ODD OTTER

One obvious odd otter
Two tickling tiny tigers
Three thinking thoughtful things
Four fierce foxes fighting for food
Five foolish fairies fidgeting for fish
Six silver shiny shaking shouting snakes
Seven stupid skateboarding skeletons
Eight eagles' eggs
Nine nibbling naughty nightingales
Ten tooting tweeties.

Charleen Meredith (8)
Carswell Primary School

ANIMALS

In a faraway place
I tie my lace
Where the elephants play
And the horses say 'Neigh'
That's where I shall stay
All day to play.

In a faraway place
I tie my lace
Where the grass is green
And the cows make cream
That's where I shall stay
All day to play.

In a faraway place
I tie my lace
Where the bears catch fish
And make a tasty dish
That's where I shall stay
All day to play.

Elisha Fiddaman (8)
Carswell Primary School

OH MR PUSSY CAT

Oh Mr Pussy Cat,
Who do you think you are?
Putting dirty footprints
All over our car.

Oh Mr Pussy Cat,
Who do you think you are?
Gobbling up your breakfast
And lying on our car.

Oh Mr Pussy Cat,
Who do you think you are?
Eating loads of cat food
We're in a bad mood.

Brittany Chandler (8)
Carswell Primary School

DARK

We were all in the bedroom
And my friends went down
The electricity turned off
And a rumble touched the ground.

My door went bang
And my bed went clang
Then a Dracula came
And left me a fang.

All went silent
Till the full moon came out
Howl went the werewolf
And my friend gave a shout.

My friends came up
And saw me in fright
And said 'Forget about it'
I was shivering all night.

Morning came
I jumped out of bed
Jumped down my ladder
And there stood Fred.

Daniella Rogers (9)
Carswell Primary School

LAUREN BRANT

L auren is my name
A nd writing poems is my game
U nderneath all the pages
R ead what I have written
E ven though you cannot see it
N ever will you see me sit and write

B eautiful writing in my book
R uin it I don't care
A fter all I love poems
N ever ever will I stop
T he fun has only just begun.

Lauren Brant (8)
Carswell Primary School

SPRING

S melly flower just growing
P eople buying bubbles that children are blowing
R eally nice blossom just going high
I t's the holidays, not time to say goodbye
N ow it's time to relax
G reat, but soon winter's back.

Gemma Harling (8)
Carswell Primary School

JUNGLE

I went on an adventure in the jungle
First I met a monkey, he was fat and chunky
Then I met a snake but I think it was fate
Soon I met a leopard, his owner was a shepherd
Then there was lightning, it was very frightening
So I went in a cave and acted brave
When it stopped I went underwater and got hit by a wave
Then I met a man called Dave, he needed a shave
I said 'Hope you don't die'
I went away and heard a cry
When it ceased I saw Dave being chased by a hairy beast.

James Bell (9)
Clifton Hampden CE Primary School

THE ZOO

I went to the zoo,
And I saw an elephant,
It looked really sad.
And then I saw a tiger
That looked very mad!
When I saw the bats
They gave me a scare,
But then I saw the red pandas
And I knew they were rare.
I looked at my map
But then I saw a crocodile go
Snap, snap!

Camilla Farrant (9)
Clifton Hampden CE Primary School

GOING THROUGH SPACE

Going through space
Is sometimes a race
Going at your own pace
See a floating star
Wondering where you are
It is a little bizarre
See the future
See the past
Sometimes going
A little too fast
When you go through space
Is it a race?
Will you wonder where you are?
It is very bizarre
See your face in space.

Catherine Curran (9)
Clifton Hampden CE Primary School

RHYME STEW

First a bit of butter
Then an ice cream tart
A drop of hot relish
And a tin of lavender polish
Twirly, whirly, twisty, long
And curled spaghetti

With just a touch of confetti
Wrinkle cream and hair cuttings
(From our dog Dream)
Sifting through the cupboard
Found some brown sauce

And a tape of Inspector Morse
An old newspaper and a pair of glasses
And two bus passes and . . .
Kaboom!
Grandma, I've got your medicine.

Elisha Riel (10)
Clifton Hampden CE Primary School

SUMMER

I am going to the park
It will never get dark
Mum said be back by nine
I haven't got the time

I'm on the swings
Eating onion rings
Thinking of my boyfriend
Then he comes round the bend

He starts to kiss me
But he gets stung by a bee
That was the end of me
The sun starts setting

It is beautiful
        lovely
                hot
                      bright

Oh the time!
I got grounded
Mum was very worried.

Terri Ann Greenaway (9)
Clifton Hampden CE Primary School

A FLOATING BOAT

A boat is sailing
Not slow or fast
They call it wailing
They say it travelled in the past
Dolphins splashing
Whales calling
Parrots bashing
People yawning
People punting
Parrots squawking
Someone hunting
People walking
Pirates saying
Cats scratching
Horse neighing
Penguins catching
Finally they land on a shore.

Melanie Farmer (9)
Clifton Hampden CE Primary School

MY KIND OF BOY

A spoonful of kindness
A drop of cheekiness
Blue eyes
Brown hair
A bucket of cleverness
A pinch of style
A touch of good looks
Stir for a few minutes to give it more flavouring
And add a sense of humour
And then serve up with gravy.

Alex Wood (10)
Clifton Hampden CE Primary School

DOUBLE BASS

A double bass is a funny old instrument
It looks like a fat guitar
It curves like my brother's brain
It has a big, fat belly like our local plumber
When you bow it, it sounds like a chainsaw madly out of control
But when you pluck it, it's more like the thumping of my heart
Yes, the double bass is a funny old instrument.

Josh Selwood (10)
Crowmarsh Gifford CE Primary School

DRUMBEATS

Drumbeats,
Standards waving,
Armour clanks at knight's charge,
Clashing swords whistling in the air,
Battle.

Henry Fletcher (10)
Crowmarsh Gifford CE Primary School

LIGHTNING

Lightning -
Dark clouds gather,
A charge of electrons,
Suddenly a flash and a roar -
It strikes.

Samuel Diserens (11)
Crowmarsh Gifford CE Primary School

THE SEVEN AGES

A baby is a tricycle needing its brakes oiling
The schoolboy is a mountain bike rushing around doing skids
A lover is a motorbike revving his engine and showing off
A college student is an old banger because he doesn't have
                                                  much money
A job is a Ferrari and you have lots of money to spend on it
A man who's near his death is a wheelchair pushing himself along
Death is a hearse taking you slowly to the funeral.

Barnaby Sayce (9)
Crowmarsh Gifford CE Primary School

THE SEVEN AGES

A baby roaring like a lioness protecting its children
A schoolgirl walking, as slow as a slug
A teenager pouncing like a proud leopard
A college girl like a sly tiger, hiding from people
A working girl is proud to be a panther, rare and special
An old man like a snail slithering its way through the grass
Near death, like an ill elephant.

Naomi Bosworth (10)
Crowmarsh Gifford CE Primary School

GRANDAD

My granddad is a rock hard chair with splinters,
Like when you wake up in the morning and your cover has fallen off.
He is a lemon as well,
He is a thunderstorm when he gets angry,
He's like a German shepherd dog.

Thomas Reed (11)
Crowmarsh Gifford CE Primary School

GRANDMA

Grandma is a soft, purring cat by the fire
A sweet, sweet, sweet strawberry glistening in the sun
She is a soft breeze floating through the clouds
Grandma is a warm armchair full of fluffy cushions all snug and cosy
A thick coating of soft, white snow just like velvet
She is a patchwork quilt spread across my bed
Grandma is a big, friendly teddy giving me a big bear hug
A soft autumn leaf drifting from the trees above
She is a twinkling star all bright by the moonlight
Grandma is the bright ray of sunlight bursting through the clouds
A gentle drop of rain trickling into the streams
She is a soft, white snowflake glistening from the sky
Grandma is a sleek dolphin with a happy heart.

Louise Bodeker (10)
Crowmarsh Gifford CE Primary School

THE SEVEN AGES

A baby is a roaring lion, its skin soft and smooth,
A schoolgirl is as slow as a snail, walking lonely to school,
The teenager is as chatty as a chimpanzee and as quick
and fast as a cheetah
A college student is as large as an elephant and as loaded as an ox
An actress is as cheerful as a monkey and as funny as a baboon
A retired lady is as crooked as a snake and as croaky as a frog
A grandma near death is as lazy as a bear, growling itself
softly to sleep.

Ceinor Sadler (10)
Crowmarsh Gifford CE Primary School

THE TITANIC

The huge liner sat in the dock,
Waiting for its cargo load of stock.
Its grey hulk rose above the sea,
Dwarfing its surroundings to the size of a pea.

The day the Titanic set sail.

When dawn arrived the people did line,
The rising sun promised it would be fine.
The cameras, the press and even the queen,
All turned up to survey the scene.

The day the Titanic set sail.

The adults stomped up waiting to see their bed,
The babies stopped crying because they were being fed.
On deck the children danced,
As they were past France.

The day the Titanic set sail.

As they glided past Spain,
They saw the Spanish train.
The adults popped champagne corks,
While the men banged their forks.

The day the Titanic set sail.

One early morning, from one end of the boat, there was a crash,
The waves they did lash.
Below deck children wept
As they leapt.

The day the Titanic set sail.

'Lower the lifeboats' called the crew,
Panic came, only to a few.
They all knew only a few would stay,
Some were rescued but only lasted a day.

The day the Titanic set sail.

**Stephanie Cummings (10)
Fir Tree Junior School**

TITANIC

The day Titanic set sail
The people looked up at the rail
To see the boat set sail
As the boat left the dock leaving its trail behind
As the crew wound the anchor, it whined

The Titanic set sail
Dolphins swimming below
As the waves splashed against the boat
The captain in the bridge house, in the log he wrote
On the deck children running
With their tops they were spinning
The day the Titanic set sail
Suddenly there was a big crash
Everything went smash
The ship snapped in half
And no one laughed
The day the Titanic sank
It was as heavy as a tank
Suddenly it just sank, people were everywhere
The day the Titanic sank.

**Tyrone Chainey (11)
Fir Tree Junior School**

THE TITANIC

The Titanic was a big, huge ship
The bagmen getting a great, big tip
Sat on the dock
Being loaded with stock
The month the Titanic set sail

The children pulled their parents along
As the staff greeted them with a song
The queen waved goodbye
As the sun shone brightly in the sky
The month the Titanic set sail

It started to get dark
As the children watched Noah's Ark
Adults at the bar
Now they had got quite far
The month the Titanic set sail

The ship sailed along the smooth sea
As some children played with a huge chickpea
Just past South France
Adults doing a slow dance
The month the Titanic set sail

People screaming
The ship started leaning
The captain saw huge ice
He knew it didn't look nice
Crash, bang, squeak, white ice

The boat was split in half
Nobody was up for a laugh
Overboard the people jumped
Fell into a lifeboat with a bump
The month the Titanic set sail

The ship began to sink
The crew cut the lifeboat's link
It lay on the seabed
A picture in people's heads
The day the Titanic sank.

Emma Chapman (11)
Fir Tree Junior School

TITANIC

In the morning people get on the boat
and will it stay up trying to float.

The Titanic will sail through the sea
but it will only seem like a tiny pea.

All the crowd waved their hats
people got on Titanic with their dogs and cats.

On that day the Titanic sailed away.

In the very pitch black of night,
they struck an iceberg, such a fright.

All in first class had things to find,
but they had to leave them all behind.

Most of the people fell to their death,
Gasping, breathed their last breath.

All the lifeboat men said are you alive
but none would get in the water with a dive.

They all knew they were going to die
and be taken to heaven in the sky.

Thomas Saunders
Fir Tree Junior School

THE TITANIC

The huge liner sat in the dock
Waiting for its stock
Its grey hulk rose above the sea
Dwarfing its surroundings to the size of a pea.
The day the Titanic set sail.

Adults and children pushing their way through,
Most people haven't got a clue.
The queen was there cheering them on
The sun was rising and it shone
The day the Titanic set sail.

The engine started to run
People were having lots of fun
They were just leaving the shore
The people who owned it shut the door
The day the Titanic set sail.

The big black and white ship started to sail away
Some people didn't have a say
Further and further it sailed away
People were having a pray
The day the Titanic set sail.

Inside the boat, men and ladies were having food
The poor men and ladies were in a mood
As the clock struck twelve they were just travelling past France
Most men and women were having a dance
The day the Titanic set sail.

Along came a massive block of ice
Everyone started to pray to Christ
Crash, bang, boom, bash
The iceberg came apart in a flash
The day the Titanic set sail.

Everyone started to cry
They all said goodbye
Hope you make it, good luck
The ship was sinking and it started to look like muck
The day the Titanic set sail.

Tell your children what I've told
Tell them when you're old
The last you saw of the Titanic.

Mickey Woods (11)
Fir Tree Junior School

THE TITANIC

The huge liner sat in the dock
Waiting for its cargo load of stock
Its grey hulk rose above the sea
Dwarfing its surroundings to the size of a pea

The day the Titanic set sail

Happy adults and children walked along the gangway
As all the children go on out to play
Adults are drinking wine
Looking as though they are fine

The day the Titanic set sail

The cameras, the press and the queen
Went to observe the scene
The crew jumped aboard
And prayed to the Lord

The day the Titanic set sail

The children went to the stage to dance
While the ship passed France
Adults popping champagne corks
To go with their dish of pork

The day the Titanic set sail

The posh looking ship
Was serving chips
For the children went early to bed
Not a tear to shed

The day the Titanic set sail

Then one dark night
Everyone woke with a fright
There was a flash
Then suddenly a splash

The night the Titanic was there

People started screaming and shouting
As the women started counting
Children burst into tears
And the passengers all had fears

The night the Titanic was there

The captain called 'Lower the lifeboats'
And put them all afloat
Women and children went first
The lifeboats nearly burst

The night the Titanic was there

As the ship began to sink
They all went under as though they blinked
Then men jumped off
The poor old ladies sat there and coughed

An amazing ship to have seen
Watched by the queen
The end of *the Titanic*.

Leanne Palmer (10)
Fir Tree Junior School

THE TITANIC

There it lay upon the sea
Unsinkable its been said to be
Giving time for the people to say farewell
Listening for the loud outgoing bell
The day the engine started

People stood and said goodbye
Their loved ones even began to cry
For the thought of them setting sail
Just in case the engine did fail
The day the engine started

The children ran up on board
Their relatives praying to the Lord
A crew member let go of the rope
Wishing and praying that he could cope
The day the engine started

They sailed across the sea
Knowing that it would be
A cold and gloomy night
Cold enough to give people a fright
The day the engine started

They enjoyed their stay
Every night and every day
Their dinner, their wine
Rich people dressed so fine
The week the engine started

They were all prancing about
Although the crew had a doubt
For they saw something ahead
'An iceberg!' the crew man said
The night the Titanic sank

The people were panicking and scared
The captain just stared
For he will have to go down with the ship
For him it's not a life remembering trip
The night the Titanic sank

The children and mums had to get on straight away
But their fathers, they had to stay
The boat was crashing into the sea
Goners that's what most of them will be
The night the Titanic sank

People risked their lives for this trip
The captain said 'It's an astonishing ship'
In the dining room the captain died
While everyone ran about terrified
The night the Titanic sank

The Titanic eventually snapped in half
The people kept on bullying the staff
To get off safely
To let them free
The night the Titanic sank

This is a sad story as you can see
It's a sinkable ship, dead the captain would be
Rely on the crew
See if it's true
The night the Titanic sank.

Lisa Nicholls (11)
Fir Tree Junior School

THE TITANIC

The huge ship sat in the dock
Waiting for lots of stock
Its grey hulk above the sea
Dwarfing its surroundings to the size of a pea
The day the Titanic set sail.

As they ran or walked aboard
As they were praying to their Lord
The people were feeling nice and kind
Just like lots of people, including the blind
The day the Titanic set sail.

The camera man, the press and even the queen
Nobody wanted to be mean
As the queen chucked champagne
As they went back through the lane
The day the Titanic set sail.

Now the day is finally here
All the dads were drinking beer
As they go and pass Spain
No one was in pain
The day the Titanic set sail.

Now the journey is finally on
As the sun brightly shone
As the children went to bed
They slept like their heads were full of lead
The day the Titanic set sail.

On the dark, cold night
Everyone woke with a fright
All they heard was smash and bash
And presumed it was a crash
The day the Titanic crashed.

Everyone was screaming and shouting
And everyone was doubting
Everyone ran to the middle of the outside of the ship
No one wanted to have a kip
They day the Titanic crashed.

As the ship began to crack
As it loses its colour black
It was going further and further into the sea
People were jumping off like me
The day the Titanic crashed.

Now all that was left was the top of the ship
As most bits were frozen like your lip
The ship has now gone into the water
Is this the end, you decide, you ought to
The day the Titanic sank.

The end, or is it?

Jake Clarke (11)
Fir Tree Junior School

The Titanic

Today is the day the Titanic set sail
The queue for tickets moves as slow as a snail
The Titanic is bigger than a boat can be
As everyone gets on they jump with glee
The Titanic is an unsinkable ship
Everyone knew it would be a very safe trip
Finally it's 12 o'clock
The time Titanic leaves the dock.

The captain is in a very good mood
Then suddenly he has a plan
To give all the guests a nice surprise
He will have to tell a few lies
If he was to increase the speed
He thinks it would be a good deed
To get to America in double quick time
He gives the workers an extra dime.

The guests don't realise they are going too fast
Suddenly the captain's glory doesn't last
An iceberg is heading straight for them
As everyone looks, it turns to mayhem
As everyone starts to try and hide
The iceberg wrecks the Titanic's side
The unsinkable ship is history
His wonderful dream is fantasy.

Water rushes around Titanic
All everyone does is panic, panic, panic
Everyone pushes right past the staff
Then the ship snaps in half
People fall in the freezing cold water
For them it feels like torture
Finally the ship does down
Some people freeze, some people drown.

The next day at the bottom of the sea
Lies the Titanic, wrecked as could be
People lay floating dead
Their families, tears they do shed
The world is affected by this terrible tragedy
As all the dead people are floating in the sea.

Kieran Bowen (11)
Fir Tree Junior School

THE TITANIC

As they load up the boat with food
Everyone's in a good mood
Staring up at the boat
Watching it float
The day the Titanic set sail

As they walked up the plank
They said their thanks
Watching the seagulls fly around
Some even landed on the ground
The day the Titanic set sail

As the people started to board
They looked like a happy hoard
Some people took dogs
Others were dancing in clogs
The day the Titanic set sail

They left the dock
At ten o'clock
They were all as happy as can be
Especially someone called Lee
They day the Titanic set sail

The days went on and on
Three had already gone
They were in a cold place
With a frozen face
The week the Titanic set sail

They were still full of fun
Even though there wasn't a sun
There were icebergs floating
Down below gamblers were gloating
The week the Titanic set sail

Suddenly there was a crash
And a very big bash
The boat split in half
There was a very nasty draught
The week the Titanic sank

The children got off first
The side boards had all burst
The people were in a panic
Everything was manic
The week the Titanic sank

The men knew they would die
The women nearly did cry
As they got off the boat
It did not float
The week the Titanic sank

Some people jumped off
Old people did cough
There was no time to waste
They hurried in haste
The week the Titanic sank

It was such a sight
People died in fright
The boat sank altogether
That's the last of it forever
The week the Titanic sank.

Emma Mundy
Fir Tree Junior School

THE TITANIC

The Titanic was a wonderful ship
The passengers couldn't wait for the trip
As the people walked on
They started to sing a song
They day the Titanic set sail

1912 was the year
The queen gave a cheer
Then she waved goodbye to the boat
Standing in her long, velvet coat
The day the Titanic set sail

The boat glided across the sea
Whilst the cooks were preparing the tea
Everyone was in the dining room
The staff were singing a tune
The day the Titanic set sail

What a week it had been
Some wonderful sights they had seen
A few at a time, they left the room
And went for a walk in the light of the moon
The week the Titanic set sail

As they went to bed
The captain's heart turned to lead
As he was whistling a tune
He saw something in the light of the moon
The week the Titanic set sail

There was a bang, there was a crash
The water made a massive splash
They all started to scream and shout
'Help, help, get the lifeboats out'
The week the Titanic set sail

The mound of ice in which they crashed
It made the boat slightly smashed
They made a rush to get away
On the boats they sailed for days

The day the Titanic sank

As the boat tore in two
The people on board fell straight through
They fell in the sea to their death
On the boat nobody was left

When the survivors got back to shore
Someone came out from a door
The next day it was headline news
The Titanic has split in two!

Jennifer Graham (10)
Fir Tree Junior School

THE TITANIC

Lots of people came to see
Just how good the Titanic would be
All the people were cheering and shouting
Because the ship was the size of a mountain
This is the best ship on the sea

All the people came on board
As the man undid a cord
All the people stopped and heard
The first propeller started to turn
This is the best ship on the sea

As the ship got out of the bay
Half of the spectators went away
When the boat got halfway out to sea
The queen said 'This is the best ship there will be
This is the best ship there will ever be'
This is the best ship on the sea

The 3rd class people went down below
They all made friends and said hello
3rd and 2nd class started to play
All of the 1st class munched away
This is the best ship on the sea

All the children got quite tired
The air outside was quite mild
They wrapped up in lots of warm clothes
An iceberg was ahead but nobody knows
This is the best ship on the sea

Bang, wallop, we just crashed
Bang, wallop, boom, smash
As the white ice floated on deck
It all made an awful mess
This is the best ship on the sea

Half of the ship filled with water
Get the lifeboats out, you know you ought to
Women and children only
Come on, careful and slowly
This is the best ship on the sea

As the nose went down deep
Children and couples fast asleep
Finally the boat snapped in half
This is serious, you shouldn't laugh
This is the best ship on the sea

Only a quarter of the people survived
Only half of the people tried
After a while the ship went under
All the people began to wonder
Why did the Titanic sink?

Luke Wood (11)
Fir Tree Junior School

THE TITANIC

The great big ship was sat on the dock
Ready for a big flock
The sun was bright
And the ship was full of light
The day the Titanic set sail

The engines started to roar
Then they shut the door
They started to be on their way
Across the bay
The day the Titanic set sail

The rich class
Went with brass
The people who were poor
Their clothes are all torn
The day the Titanic set sail

They'd gone miles and miles and were nowhere near land
They passed beaches with golden sand
The ship was riding on the wide ocean
Lots of people were doing a motion
The week the Titanic sank

A wallop, crash, bang
The ship sounded as hollow as a can
The huge ship carried along the sea
The size of a pea
The week the Titanic sank

The boat started to sink
And all of the drink turned to ink
They shouted all the boats out
The captain had a big doubt
The week the Titanic sank

He shouted women and children first
And a man looked like he was going to burst
All the boats were used up
People started to throw cups
The week the Titanic sank

Most of the men were trying to jump aboard
They pushed all of the things which were stored
The boat has snapped, they're going to die
And it's time to say goodbye
The day the Titanic sank.

Francesca McGuinness (10)
Fir Tree Junior School

THE TITANIC

The huge liner sat in the dock
Waiting for its cargo load of stock
Its grey hulk rose above the sea
Dwarfing its surroundings to the size of a pea
The first puff

When the people arrived at the dock
It sounded like birds of a flock
The people all in a line
The sun promised it would be fine
The second puff

The cameras, press and queen
Trotted up to look at the scene
As the children began to dance
They sailed passed France
The third puff

Then some children were playing
As adults were in their beds laying
Then everyone stopped and heard a crash
Then there was a big bash
The fourth puff

Then they hit an iceberg
The captain was called McBurg
Then the ladies got their child
As the parents didn't feel mild
The fifth puff

The water came up deep
As the children awoke from their sleep
Then the children started with a fright so they had to go
As they came from below
The sixth puff

As the ding stayed still
The adults kneeled, they prayed they wouldn't be killed
As the children cried
They thought their parents would die
The seventh puff

As the boat snapped in half
They just forgot about the craft
Then the Titanic sank like lead
As people panicked the blood came out red
The last puff.

Charlotte Douglas-Gilbert (10)
Fir Tree Junior School

THE TITANIC

The huge liner ship sat in the dock
While time seemed like it would not tock
Its big, grey body was really high
While all the people were saying goodbye
The Titanic is about to set sail

The Titanic set off on its trip
And so all the crabs had nothing to nip
All the children had so much fun
Eating all the freshly cooked buns
The Titanic has set sail

Then the crew saw an iceberg
While a passenger was complaining at Captain Surg
Suddenly there was a big bump
And the lady stopped having mumps
The Titanic had set sail

Then with a fright the boat had stopped
And all the crew started to mop
The water had started creeping in
While people were floating in bins
The Titanic had stopped

The queues got longer to get out the boat
While the crew put dinghies afloat
All the children went first
While the crew had problems with dinghies that burst
The Titanic had stopped

All the people had got off the boat
While some dinghies would not float
Then the boat snapped in half
And how some wished that they were at home in a bath
The Titanic had sunk.

Sarah Morris (9)
Fir Tree Junior School

THE TITANIC

The thought of the ship made you shiver
It really made the tourists quiver

Titanic is the biggest ship there ever was
It could sail to any place, even the Greek island Kos

At last the people were on the Titanic
No more queuing, we don't have to panic

The ship set off with a very loud roar
The ship was ready to go on the world tour

The ship's speed rose to 80 miles an hour
The Titanic's force was as big as a tower

All the water splashed into the boat
It was a good job everyone was wearing a coat

That night when everybody went to bed
All the people had a dread

Smash went the lights
They woke up with a fright

Crash, bang, wallop
They had crashed into some ice
Now all the passengers didn't feel that nice

Now the ship was broken in half
There wasn't any single laugh

People dying in the freezing cold sea
The water was so cold, it felt like you had been stung by a bee

Titanic was a big tragedy
Now it's lying at the bottom of the sea.

Jonathan Smith (11)
Fir Tree Junior School

THE TITANIC

The day the Titanic boat sailed to sea
The surroundings around the boat were as small as a pea
The queen was standing waving
The men stood shaving
The day Titanic set to sea

The day all the kids ran up the steps with speed
The people below looked as small as a seed
Their mums and dads looked very shocked
When they got on the boat stood docked
The day Titanic set to sea

All the blokes were wearing sharp ties
All the kids were telling big lies
All the boys were having lunch
All the girls were having a munch
The day the Titanic set to sea

The boat was pulling out of dock
The people were looking at the clock
The engine left a trail
And all the people looked pale
The day the Titanic set to sea

Off it set to go on a journey
All the captains were very early
Half of the journey was very nice
All the rich people were able to eat rice
The day Titanic set to sea

Then everything went wrong
The people stopped singing their songs
Bang, wallop, bash, what was that?
Oh no, my hat!
That was the day Titanic sank.

'Oh no, it's a big white bit of ice'
One hit and the deck was sliced
All of a sudden children getting on their coats
And hurrying onto the lifeboats
The day Titanic sank

Some people nearly survived
All the others into the sea they died
The boat was suddenly gone
All the lifeboats went on

Oh no, the boat was gone
All the lifeboats went on
Oh, what a story this is
The boat was such a whiz
The day Titanic was gone.

Keeley Green (10)
Fir Tree Junior School

THE TITANIC

There once was a boat called Titanic
Its sister was called Britannic
It sat in the dock
Not aware of the shock
The week the Titanic set sail.

The people looked as small as seeds
The Titanic was doing a good deed
The Titanic set sail in the sea
They saw some boats, they looked as small as peas
The day the Titanic set sail.

The men were all talking
The women were all walking
The kids were eating cake
The parents were having a break
The week the Titanic set sail.

The children were sleeping
The parents were peeping
So the parents could go under the stars
They played some darts
The day the Titanic set sail.

Suddenly they saw the ice
The man dropped the bowl of rice
The unsinkable ship began to sink
People would not blink
The week the Titanic set sail.

Some people were dying
Some people were crying
The surviving people swam to the boat
Then the people set afloat
The week the Titanic set sail.

Robbie Grant (10)
Fir Tree Junior School

THE TITANIC

The huge liner sat in the dock
Waiting for its cargo load of stock
Its grey hulk rose above the sea
Dwarfing its surroundings to the size of a pea
The day the Titanic set sail.

The queen was there cheering them on
As the yellow sun put them on
The children were running like it was funny
The ladies were eating honey
The day the Titanic set sail.

We went past France
And did a little dance
As we went past Spain
It started to rain
The week the Titanic set sail.

As the children were sleeping
The couples were creeping
To steal a kiss under the star
While their partner was at the bar
The week the Titanic set sail.

A crack as loud as a horse being whipped
A hole appeared in the deck of the ship
Lower the lifeboats called the crew
Panic set in, calm stayed with only a few
The week the Titanic sank.

Chrissie Atkins (9)
Fir Tree Junior School

THE TITANIC

The Titanic was a massive boat,
amazing that it would ever float.
First class, second class, third class,
It shone as if it were glass.
the day the Titanic set sail
the day the Titanic set sail.

One very fine day,
It went far away -
the size of it,
the size of it.
the day the Titanic set sail,
the day the Titanic set sail.

In the dead of night,
a terrible sight -
upon the big Titanic,
it was a major panic
the day the Titanic set sail,
the day the Titanic set sail.

They hit it very fast,
it would never be in the past
they hit an iceberg,
they hit an iceberg.
the day the Titanic set sail,
the day the Titanic set sail.

Some people got in a lifeboat,
lucky some could float,
some people survived,
but some people died.
the day the Titanic set sail,
the day the Titanic set sail.

Paris Sandiford (10)
Fir Tree Junior School

TITANIC

As the Titanic stood tall and proud,
Everyone gathered and made a crowd.
In the autumn's breezy blow,
The lines began to grow and grow.

Luggage was taken to the boat,
Everyone had wrapped up warm in a coat.
Now they were ready, the boat was untied,
Most of the children wept and cried.

On went the people, on the greatest boat of all,
They were looking forward to the buffet and the ball.
Out in the ocean and further away,
The sun came out and it felt like May.

On the water the boat bobbed about,
The captain began to shout and shout.
They'd hit an iceberg, what should they do?
What an awful hullabaloo.

The boat began to split in two,
None of them knew what to do.
This wasn't the time to joke and laugh,
One of the people nearly split in half.

Out came the lifeboats and rescued some,
The others panicked but tried to hum.
People jumped in but died of cold,
On the sea floor they began to mould.

Verity Graham (9)
Fir Tree Junior School

TITANIC

In the dock the ship lay
The greatest boat they all say.
Finest cups and silver all around
The best china ever found
The day the ship set sail.

The bustling people filled the dock
Cases, clothes, cars and stock.
Then the food crates got carried in
Making the dock look as small as a pin
The day the ship set sail.

The bustling people ran past
The poor people always last.
The men and women waved their hats
Bringing on dogs and cats
The day the ship set sail.

The boat at last was in the ocean
Bumping on waves a steady motion.
The steam engine going as fast as it could
The grand Titanic made of metal and wood
The day the ship set sail.

The boat sailed for a few days
Making its path in many ways.
Floating in the icy cold
The boat kept going it could not hold
The day the ship set sail.

In one afternoon it did suddenly strike
A hole appeared on the side, it was a fright.
'We are all going to die,' they cried
They all tried to get upstairs to hide
The day the ship set sail.

All the people lower down drowned
They were never again found.
Women rushed to lifeboats
People in the water tried to keep afloat
The day the ship set sail.

At last the ship sank
People held onto plank.
All the people in the sea did die
Frozen and perished where they did lie
The day the Titanic sank!

Nicholas Field (9)
Fir Tree Junior School

The Titanic

When they made the boat
It was such a float,
The size of it,
The size of it,
The day that it set sail.

In the morning of one day,
The Titanic sailed far away,
Along the seas along it went,
It was so so pleasant,
The day that it set sail.

The 15th of October,
People were very sober
There was a lot to do,
And people shouted, 'Where are you?'
The day that it set sail.

The people always got food,
So they were never in a mood,
Always wanting more and more,
Never ever going to be poor,
The day that it set sail.

Going into the Antarctic,
Everyone thought they were going thick,
Going into an iceberg on the ice,
They all had to rub their eyes twice
The day that it set sail.

The boat was sinking into the water,
The men said, 'Jump overboard daughter,'
'Come on mate,'
'Come on mate,'
The day that it set sail.

The people went and froze to death,
After five seconds they ran out of breath,
The lightning struck,
The lightning struck,
The day the Titanic sank!

Demi Reid (10)
Fir Tree Junior School

The Titanic

The Titanic was a black and white huge ship
And all the bags men were given big tips
She sat in the dock
Waiting for her stock
    Looking so dazzling
The queen christened the boat
Titanic set afloat
The crew were singing a song
Whilst the Titanic moved along
    Looking so dazzling
The children were all laughing
The men were all bathing
The engines were burning
And all the propellers are turning
    Looking so dazzling
All the posh people were wearing ties
The poor people were telling big lies
Chandeliers shining so bright
The cabins were filled with a little light
    Looking so dazzling
The rich people lived luxurious lives
They all had very nice wives
The poor people had a bad, bad time
They didn't even own a diary
    Looking so dazzling
The two men in the crows nest
Saw a figure
One of the men with a gun knew
He was dead so he pulled the trigger
Water flooded the deck,
It was up to people's necks
    Looking so dazzling

The unsinkable began to sink
The crew cut the lifeboat links
The children and women went first
The brig smashed and burst
    Looking so dazzling
Thousands of people died
Lots of people are still alive
The survivors swam
To the nearest boat and set afloat.
    Looking so dazzling.
And now it lays on the sea bed
Thousands of people are still dead.
    Looking so rusty.

Liam Johnson (10)
Fir Tree Junior School

THE TITANIC

Shining in the dock, silver and gold
People doing the last checks on the ship
It waits to sail, it will never be sold
People running around, there was a snip.

Smoke coming from the funnel, people are ready to sail
'All aboard,' people shouted, lots of boxes and cars loaded on it
The people were on, it sailed off as fast as a snail
People checking the clothes even swimming kits.

People playing games jumping up and down
The ship was going faster than it is ever
People looking at the sky, it was going brown
The people sat on the chair, they were leather.

It happened, they hit an iceberg in the night
People were running around the ship, up, down the stairs
People were shouting, it was anything but light
People were running around, it was as busy as a fair.

Water was rushing in, people screaming for their life
The end of the Titanic was splitting off the front of the ship
Cars, boxes, cases, even a knife
Water was still pouring in, people were trying to get some kip.

The Titanic was sinking to the bottom of the sea
People jumped into the sea, they saw the captain's bed
The captain stayed on the ship, he was looking at a painting of a bee
It was a bad day for the Titanic, it was dead.

Jake Brown (11)
Fir Tree Junior School

BOGEYMAN

There's a bogeyman in the bathroom,
He doesn't know what he's for,
I hear the floorboards creaking,
As he walks across the floor.

He moans in the night,
He groans in the day,
My sister and I do hope
He soon will go away.

There was a bogeyman in the bathroom,
But now those times are through,
I really am relieved
That he's gone to stay with you.

James Logan (9)
Marcham CE Primary School

THE RUMBLE

They were in the ring and ready to rumble,
Then the bell went, what a bundle.
A right hand from The Rock,
A left hand from Austin,
Kane got out and got a dustbin.
He got back in and hit them with the bin,
He picked The Rock and chokeslammed him.
Austin got up and stunned them both,
Then he stood up and called for the beer,
He just ended The Rock's career.

Chris Tolley (10)
Marcham CE Primary School

IF I RULED THE WORLD...

If I ruled the world
I would make a giant straw
To suck up all the bad things;
Crime, jealousy and war.

All litter would be recycled
And put into a bin
The environment would stay clean
And to drop rubbish would be a sin.

The air would be free from pollution
And the only thing left in the sky
Would be choruses of notes gliding through the air
From a bird singing way up high.

I would make power spark from my fingertips
And hurricanes would cease
Earthquakes would come to a halt
And the world would live in peace.

Rachael Dredge (11)
Marcham CE Primary School

THE LOVE BUG

Love is red and purple too
It smells like roses, pink and blue
The taste is out of this world
The sound is like some dropping pearls
It feels like cuddly fur
It lives in the heart where it purrs.

Jos Rowe
Marcham CE Primary School

NIGHT

Monsters lurking
Werewolves working
All night long.

The moon replaces the sun
The stars twinkle for fun
All night long.

People sleep
Hedgehogs peep
All night long.

Cats prowl
Bears growl
All night long.

But there is a fight
Of day and night
At dawn.

Hannah Fathers (8)
Marcham CE Primary School

HOPE

Hope is yellow
It smells like honeysuckle
Hope tastes like sweet creamy fudge
It sounds like butterflies flapping their wings
Hope feels smooth and fluffy
Hope lives in your beating heart.

Elizabeth Bell (10)
Marcham CE Primary School

BLACKBIRD

A little crack in the shell
As his mother stares and waits.
One day he'll be flying over
Walls and roofs and gates.

His parents fly back and forth
Bringing worms and slugs.
When he's older and wants a snack
He'll find himself some bugs.

An orange beak and feathers black
He glides above the trees.
As night-time falls he sings his song
And roosts amongst the leaves.

Madeleine Dyer (9)
Marcham CE Primary School

WWF POEM

It's getting tense in the ring.
A punch, a bang and everything.
Rock bottom stone-cold stunner.
Look at Kurt, Angle, he's done a runner.
The Kane just chokeslammed The Rock.
Mankind came in and choked him with a sock.
Left hand by Rock, right hand by Austin.
Kane came in with a dustbin,
Hit The Rock on the head.
'Oh my God, he's dead!'

Sebastian Crowley (10)
Marcham CE Primary School

PLAYSTATION

When I'm on my PlayStation
I wrestle with the best
I throw them all around the ring
In my very best vest.

I drive all over the country
Over hill and mountainsides
When I smash the car to bits
I have to go and hide.

Then my mum shouts me
And I pack it all away
It's now time for my tea
What a good game I must say.

Charlie Newman (9)
Marcham CE Primary School

CAT ATTACK

Sleek black fur, shiny and soft,
Creeping about in the dusty old loft,
Sitting . . . waiting to pounce on his prey,
Lovely little kitten people might say.

Running around chasing a mouse,
Then goes in to rest in his house,
Curling up really small,
After playing with his woollen ball.

Ashley Richardson (10)
Marcham CE Primary School

WWF RAP

It's time for the match, ready to rumble,
Ouch! Bang! Scratch!
Fighting in the ring, all in a bundle,
A stunner from Austin, rock bottom from The Rock,
But Mankind came in and choked them with the sock
The match is over, what a rumble!

Fred Gardner (9)
Marcham CE Primary School

THERE ONCE WAS A MAN IN A ROCKET

There once was a man in a rocket,
Who could only just fit in your pocket
He flew up in the sky,
So high that he died,
That mad little man in a rocket!

Lauren Gardner (11)
Marcham CE Primary School

DEATH!

Death is bright red.
It feels like a hard, cold penny.
It sounds like somebody drinking.
It tastes like black coal.
It lives under the dark damp floorboards.

Stacey Greenough (10)
Marcham CE Primary School

THE COMET

Streaking through the pitch-black sky,
Travelling soundly, look at it fly!

Far, far away, out in space,
Shooting fast, at its own pace.

There it goes, out of sight,
Moving throughout the night.

Rebecca Marsh (10)
Marcham CE Primary School

ANGER

Anger is blazing hot,
It smells like mouldy cheese,
It tastes like rotten banana skins,
It sounds like a fire crackling,
It feels like sticky goo,
It lives in a firey volcano.

Alex Turney (9)
Marcham CE Primary School

THE HAMSTER

The small lazy creature
Scurrying round on its wheel,
Hardly ever stopping,
Sweet, cuddly, smooth and silky.

Sophie Hopgood (10)
Marcham CE Primary School

COLOURS

Red is burning,
Gleaming, glistening,
Crimson, ruby,
Orange is coming.

Orange is flaring,
Crystal clear,
Amber, sandy,
Yellow is near.

Yellow is glossy,
Shining, dazzling,
Buttercup, gold,
Green is advancing.

Green is lustrous,
Reflective, bright,
Jade of emerald,
Blue prepares for flight.

Blue is quivering,
Twitching, shuddering,
Sapphire, turquoise,
Purple is preening.

Purple is dominant,
Perfect, polished,
Lilac, violet,
Black is now dead.

Black is dying,
Unlit, moonless,
Ebony, inky,
The only thing colourless.

Sarah Narramore (11)
Marcham CE Primary School

THE NO LUCK DUCK

There was a young duck
Who had no good luck
He fell in a dustbin
And sat on a sharp pin
His eyes went all googely
His wings went all woogely
Oh that poor young duck
That had no good luck.

Scott Walker (11)
Marcham CE Primary School

DEATH

Death is red,
It smells like a pig sty,
Death tastes like rotten banana skins,
It sounds like a hundred screams in a dark room,
It feels like slime dripping all over you,
Death lives in a creepy cave.

Emily Upjohn (9)
Marcham CE Primary School

ANGER

Anger is blazing hot,
It smells like bones with sticky gooze all over them,
It looks like a burning hot lava monster,
It feels like a dead disgusting man,
It lives at the bottom of fiery hell!

Ross Walker (9)
Marcham CE Primary School

THE WOOD

I go into the wood,
Trees are scattered here and there,
A stray mushroom
And flowers everywhere.

The winds blow gently,
There is flower scent in the air,
The day is quite a clear one,
Bright, clear and fair.

Then a neigh from nearby,
From a horse, or pony, or mare,
I wonder if I should ride him,
I wonder if I should dare.

Ellen Walton (9)
Marcham CE Primary School

FIRE

The raging fire sweeps through the starry sky
Red, orange and blue
No one can stop it
Except me or you.
Tiny specs of silver
Float past your closed eyelashes
The match that was the source of this
Is lying in an empty dish.

Matthew Ward (11)
Marcham CE Primary School

BACON SANDWICH

Pig wakes up,
Pig is bright,
Shut the door and bolt it tight,
Pig gets out
And hurts his hoof,
Shut the door and mend the roof,
Tins of meat he is for certain,
He is bound to see his final curtain
Pig says goodbye
And gets his hat,
That is life,
So that is that.

Gemma Cade (8)
Marcham CE Primary School

THE LITTLE FISH

The little fish swam,
Swim, swim, swim.
The little fish splashed,
Splash, splash, splash,
Right to the end of the pond.

The little frog jumped,
Jump, jump, jump,
The little frog hopped,
Hop, hop, hop,
Then splash, into the pond.

Sarah Waterhouse (9)
Marcham CE Primary School

My Cartoon Character

My cartoon character is a cool kid,
Everyone calls him the coolest kid in town,
He has a cool skateboard,
He has everything in his pocket,
From a hankie to a cord.
He was going to give his girlfriend a locket
But he left it in his pocket.

Alicia Simmons (10)
Marcham CE Primary School

The Rabbit

He's there, he's there, he's always aware,
But the food just never comes.
He's in his cage all day and night.
His room is overflowing, from the endless days of waiting,
For his room to be cleaned out, but the boy never comes.
But then one lonely night the wood snapped,
And all the waste fell out.
There was not a hole to escape from.
He kicked and kicked but the pile would not budge.
He remembered the old days when he was cuddled,
And played with but that was the old days.
He heard a creak, the door was opened.
It was the boy.
He walked and got some food and opened the cage door.
He shoved the food in and said, 'A pet is *not* for life!'

Richard Collinson (10)
Moulsford Preparatory School

THE SWEET SHOP

The sweet shop is a lovely place,
A place where I can go.
With black and yellow streamers out,
You never can say no.
But when I get inside of course,
The picture will just change.
The black and yellow streamers, no?
The place looks nicely strange.
The liquorice on the wall, oh yes,
The blackjacks by the door,
Some 'weathereds' on the counter, yum,
But there's still lots on the floor.
The mice that run around the shop,
They're so sweet I just can't stop.
Eating, eating all day long,
Singing my nice sweety song.
But then I see the jelly beans,
I say, oh goody, good.
I start to eat and eat and eat,
Because the beans are nice and sweet.
The ice creams are a good thing too,
They help me cool my tongue.
But soon I have to go, uh oh,
I ask for just one more.
My mother drags me out again,
Goodbye to that sweet store.
She says you're going to another place,
I think oh goody, good,
I sit back in the car, hee hee,
But when you get to the other place
It's the dentists, that's for me!

James Newman (11)
Moulsford Preparatory School

THE BEST FAMILY

The thing I love the most is the loving nature of my family.

My mum met my dad at a disco on the RAF camp
and they've been married for twenty-five years.

Six years later came my sister, it was their first child,
something was wrong with her, what could it be?
There was the smell of despair in the air,
later the doctors discovered that she had rett syndrome.

Then came me a little bit later,
and I've been late for everything else since.

Recently Benny the dog joined our family after being dumped,
our friend found him dumped outside and now he is ours.

Ours is the best family in the world.

Leigh Anderson (11)
Moulsford Preparatory School

HUNGRY VINNIE

Rhodesian ridgebacks are beautiful dogs,
The Rhodesian people love these dogs,
But these dogs are not liked by all.
The smaller dogs for instance hate these beautiful dogs,
This all starts with Vinnie.

Vinnie was a big dog,
A big dog with an appetite,
He needed something big to eat,
He needed something bigger to eat,
For he was getting bigger.

So Vinnie looked and looked and seeked
And then he saw a poodle
He ran and ran and then . . . gulp!
Vinnie ate.
That was the poodle's fate!

James Ralphs (10)
Moulsford Preparatory School

A DAY OF SUMMER

I looked up at the sky,
And saw the shining sun.
The white and fluffy clouds,
Floating silently along.

The lambs are skipping by,
The flowers blossom and look like icing.
I look up at the fruit trees,
And the fruit looks so enticing.

The bees are buzzing loudly,
They never seem to stop.
The children are splashing in the pool,
There is no one in the shops.

They are all out relaxing,
Sunbathing on the beach.
No one here is working,
Teachers do not have to teach.

So this is my poem,
I tried to make it rhyme.
I hope that you like it,
I think it sums up summertime.

Rory Van Zwanenberg (11)
Moulsford Preparatory School

My Dog

There are all types of dogs, big and small,
But there is one that's the best of all.
She is not a poodle, not a collie,
But a small clever type of doggie.

During the night she creeps upstairs,
When you get up she's never there.
In the morning she wants her food,
The owner's not up yet, time to brood.

One hour later she wants a run,
Then she remembers she has got a empty tum.
At last, he comes downstairs,
She greets him with some angry glares.

In the woods she smells a rabbit,
She's so fast she's bound to grab it.
A while later she puts up a pheasant,
Umm, pheasant pie, how pleasant!

Time to go home, cold, wet but happy,
Surely it's time for her biscuits and Chappie.
She lies by the fire, no longer chilly,
What a day for my dog called Tilly.

William Greenslade (10)
Moulsford Preparatory School

Music Is Not Bad At All

Music is not bad at all,
If you think so, you're a fool!
Music is of course the best,
And of course will pass the test!

Rap is cool,
Rock is wicked,
We scream and shout,
We jump about,
We let everyone know what it's about.

Charlie Macdonald (10)
Moulsford Preparatory School

MY DOG

My dog, all brown and white,
As brown as chocolate.
As white as the clouds in a blue sky,
As soft as butter.
All curled up on the sofa,
Playing with the other dog as fierce as fire,
Asleep on the sofa one minute,
Running like a loony the next.

Then there's shooting on frosty mornings,
Running through bushes,
Birds flying.
The smell of gunpowder,
The banging of the guns.
Then I see a fox,
A fox,
The dreaded fox.
I send the dog,
The fox runs,
I call my dog,
I hear a shot,
The fox is dead.
Oh how I love my dog.

William Emmett (11)
Moulsford Preparatory School

JOBS

The time, the time,
Oh what is the time,
Oh please tell me the time.
As this is too painful for me.

Stop!
Please stop,
But the answer is always no.
Please, no please,
Just please may I go home.

The noise, the noise,
Please stop the noise.
The bustling on the street is deafening,
The noise is irritating my mind.

The work, the work,
This work is hard,
Even too hard for me.
There's so much work,
There's too much work for me.

Sam Fletcher (10)
Moulsford Preparatory School

THE PERFECT WORLD

This is a world,
A world that is bare,
There is no city,
Just grass and privet.

This is a paradise,
A paradise for all.
You can rule,
And be a fool.

This is a world,
A world for everyone.
For ladies and gentlemen,
Boys and girls.

This is a world,
A world where everything is perfect.
Bad is good
And good is good.

Gus Bartholomew (11)
Moulsford Preparatory School

CATS

Cats prowl silently,
From door to door,
Climb onto your roof,
And drop down to the floor.

In the black of night,
Cats disappear,
Cats stealthily slip in the darkness,
In the drop of a silver tear.

Cats have nine lives,
Some people say,
They are mousers by nature,
By night but not by day.

Cats come to festivals,
Especially in May,
To scavenge for food,
But never do they stay.

Joshua Chew (10)
Moulsford Preparatory School

ANIMALS

Animals can be big and small,
Like the elephant and the ant.
Animals can be fast or slow,
Like the leopard and the cat.

Animals can be dangerous or safe,
Like the lion and the mouse.
Animals can swim or walk,
Like the shark and the plouse.

Animals can be pets or wild,
Like the crocodile and the dog.
Animals can be fat or thin,
Like the hippo and the snake.

Animals can be short or long,
Like the whale and the stag.
Animals can fly or fall,
Like the eagle and the bear.

Dominic Rothbarth (11)
Moulsford Preparatory School

FIREWORKS

A firework blossoms in the sky like a flower
It makes a big bang with all its power.

The colours are so rich and warm
It spreads out like a bee swarm.

Rockets, bangers and Catherine wheel
Sound of sizzling, crackling, welding steel,
They shoot up so fast into the sky,
Catching attention from all nearby.

Jack Barker (10)
Moulsford Preparatory School

Skiing

Skiing is fun on your own,
Skiing is even more fun with friends,
Skiing down the mountain at an exhilarating speed,
You do not know what to expect,
When other people fall over its hilarious,
But when you fall over it's not so funny.
The fact that in some ways it's dangerous
                            makes it even more fun.
Going over jumps is the best thing of all,
You can go really high,
When you take the chairlift to the top
The views can be breathtaking,
Overall skiing is great fun.

Chris Watts (10)
Moulsford Preparatory School

The Koala Bear

A koala bear has short and neat hair.
It starts to fear when people come near.
It eats the leaves of luscious green trees.
It feels the heat of the land with its feet.
The bush fire is its worst foe when it sees it
                            it's not slow to go.
It has a big black nose so it's not hard to tell
                            if they're friends or foes.
As it lives up the trees and smell of eucalyptus oils
You'll never find one with the scent of soils.
When it's a baby it lives in its mother's pouch
When it grows older its mother says, 'Ouch!'

Joe Jones (10)
Moulsford Preparatory School

YOUR MAMA IS YOUR BEST FRIEND

Your mama is your best friend
She understands what you do
It doesn't matter if you're lonely
Your mama will listen to you.

She will give you a shoulder to cry on
When you are feeling down
She will share your joy and laughter
And smooth away your frown.

Your mama will always be there
Her love will never end
No matter what you do
Your mama is your best friend.

Alexandra Hopkinson (10)
Rupert House School

THE SEAGULLS

They clasp the bread with greedy beaks
Over the seven seas they seek
Riding on
White horse peaks.

The sea beneath them deeply roars
They always search for more and more
And like rockets
Up they soar.

Emma Gibbs (10)
Rupert House School

CARING FOR PEOPLE

Doctors care for people like you
They make us all as good as new.
Being a doctor is what I wanna be
So I'm going to sit a medical degree.

I think I'd like to learn dermatology
Or perhaps I'll study oncology.
Doctors work hard and I'd like to say
That they deserve plenty of pay!

I'm going to follow my parents' footsteps
I'd rather be a GP than a medical rep.
I'd like to help the rich and the poor
And I'd love to discover an exciting new cure.

Emily Granger (9)
Rupert House School

MY FAVOURITE ANIMALS

My favourite animals are dogs
They run and play and chase frogs

My favourite animal is a horse
They walk, trot, canter and gallop but I still love them of course

My favourite animal is a cat
They like the night and they chase rats

My favourite animals are bugs
Well, there's nothing to say about them much
but all I know is some live under plugs!

Alexandra Boardman (9)
Rupert House School

THE MORNING RUSH HOUR

The dog barks at the cat
And the cat hisses and spits
Mum bellows to us 'Get dressed!'
But I've got nothing clean that fits!

My sister spills milk on the floor
My dad hides his head in the paper
My brother's still snoring in bed
And the time is getting later and later!

My puppy is chewing my homework
I'm worried I'll lose a star
My brother's just got out of bed
And mummy's revving the car.

My daddy groans at the bills
The car's now refusing to start
And mummy's going ballistic
And it's way past our time to depart.

My brother complains he's hungry
My sister smashes a plate
My dad's tearing his hair out
And my mum is screaming 'We're late!'

We bundle ourselves in the car
And mummy drives us away
The morning rush hour is over
But it'll start the very next day!

Jennifer Taylor (9)
Rupert House School

RUPERT HOUSE SCHOOL CUDDLY TEDDY BEARS

Ten cuddly teddy bears sitting in a line,
One toppled over and then there were nine.

Nine cuddly teddy bears looking what everyone ate,
One didn't feel well and then there were eight.

Eight cuddly teddy bears living in Devon,
One moved house and then there were seven.

Seven cuddly teddy bears wanting some pick 'n' mix,
One went out to the shop and then there were six.

Six cuddly teddy bears looking at a hive,
One got stung and then there were five.

Five cuddly teddy bears locked the bedroom door,
One jammed his little finger and then there were four.

Four cuddly teddy bears climbing up a tree,
One fell off a branch and then there were three.

Three cuddly teddy bears looking at an igloo,
One fell through the ice and then there were two.

Two cuddly teddy bears sitting in the sun,
One got sunburnt and then there was one.

One cuddly teddy bear working out a sum,
Then he gave up and then there were none.

Alexandra Barbour (9)
Rupert House School

EVACUEE

I remember the war began
I thought it would be lots of fun
To be evacuated away
I thought it would be like a holiday!

But when it was time to say goodbye
I started to tremble, I started to cry
I didn't want to leave mum and dad
I had never ever been so sad!

When we got to the countryside
I found that all my tears had dried
We had to stand in the village hall
With our backs against the wall!

Some people came to pick us out
I just wanted to scream and shout
We shouldn't be picked out like this
I thought of all the people I'd miss!

Finally the war was done
I'd had everything but fun . . .

Eleanor Hollier (10)
Rupert House School

THE NEW ARRIVAL

I remember,
My dad ringing up,
Telling me good news,
That I had a new baby sister!

I kept on repeating,
'A baby sister!'
Then I said,
'I want to go see her!'

Yippee! Yippee!
I couldn't wait to see her,
I was so happy,
I danced with sheer joy!

I remember,
Holding her,
In my arms,
So soft!

Emma Collinson (9)
Rupert House School

THE SINKING SUN

I remember
> The sun setting
> The water lapping against the sand
> As people said cheery goodbyes
> I gazed around the misty land.

I remember
> As I picked up my last shell
> The hum of mosquitoes nearby
> Told me that I should be in bed
> As homewards the seagulls fly

I remember
> The happiness of children
> And the sunset against a pink sky
> And the warm water lapping
> And the children saying 'Goodbye!'

Emily Shawcross (11)
Rupert House School

HAMSTERS

I'm furry and fat
I don't like their cat!
My owner must clean out my cage
I sleep all day
But come out to play
At night when I chew up a page
I chew up my hoard
Of food when I'm bored
I clean myself all on my own
When I run away
I hope I'm not prey
For the cat that will spit
Out my bones!

Charly Halsall (9)
Rupert House School

I GET ALL . . .

I get all mucky
When I feed my small ducky

I get all dirty
When I ride my horse Berty

I get all messy
When I feed my dog Jessy

I get all muddy
When I play with my buddy

My mum is so mean
She thinks I should be clean!

Davina Collas (9)
Rupert House School

MEMORIES ARE LIKE VIDEOS

Memories are like videos
In your mind
For you can watch them
Over and over again
You can replay the special moments in life
And erase the horrible ones

You can select your favourite mind movies
Like selecting movies on Sky Digital
You can cringe at the embarrassing ones
And laugh at the funny bits
Sniffle into a pillow at the sad parts

Memories are so much
Better than forgetting.

Sarah Richards (10)
Rupert House School

SCHOOL'S OUT!

Lessons, lessons, what a pain
Lessons, lessons, use your brain
Homework, homework, what a yawn
Homework, homework, up till dawn
School bus, school bus, yellow and red
School bus, school bus, what a dread
Home time, home time, home at last
Home time, home time is a blast!

Louisa Baczor (10)
Rupert House School

MEMORIES OF WHEN I WAS YOUNG

When I was young
I sucked my thumb
I really tried to stop
but I could not do it
Though I tried not to chew it
I liked it such a lot!

Then my mum
put vinegar on my thumb
from a bottle a drop
she would moisten,

but because I forgot
I could not read one jot
I thought it
said *poison!*

I have never sucked my thumb since!

Jessica Mace (8)
Rupert House School

HOUND HUNTING

Wafting, shifting smells go by
Up the staircase to the sky
Familiar smells that make you sigh
Onion smells that make you cry

Floating, gloating smells go round
Down the staircase to the ground
Moving past without a sound
Till they reach the big bloodhound.

Larissa Batt (10)
Rupert House School

MEMORIES OF THE HAUNTED INN IN HENLEY

There is an inn in Henley,
It is very spooky and old,
And inside might be a ghostly ghost,
Or so I have been told!

I've never actually seen him,
But I guess he is really there,
Because I once remember,
Hearing footsteps on the stairs!

I hoped it might be the ghost,
Of Rupert, a handsome prince,
I thought I saw his shadow,
But I've never seen him since!

Victoria Williams-Gray (9)
Rupert House School

WEEPING WILLOW

The weeping willow's long, thin branches
Fall like a maze
Of green curtains
The leaves drizzle down and float
Like tiny sailing boats
The water takes them down the river
Far, far away.

Weeping willow crying
    Green tears
Into the cold stream.

Annie Elphick (10)
Rupert House School

THE HORSE

I am a very grumpy horse
I'll bite people I don't like, of course.

I hate to canter, I hate to trot
I love to stay and eat a lot.

I love to buck, maybe to bolt
I always have since I was a colt.

I am rather lazy and just munch hay
I won't earn my keep by being ridden all day.

One day I met a gorgeous mare
She had lovely, long, smooth horse hair.

She always did shows, she loved being good
Exactly the way that I think I should.

Now, after seeing the gorgeous mare
I've learnt to be kind and to share.

    Just like you should.

Katherine Innes (9)
Rupert House School

NO BULLIES

There are no bullies in our school
Not one bully you will find
It's safe to play in the playground
As everyone is nice and kind

No one steals your break here
No one calls you names
No one whispers behind your back
Or takes your stuff for games

If you have lost a pencil
Or can't find your text book
People will be nice to you
They'll come and help you look

There are no bullies in our school
So you have nothing to fear
Because we help each other
It's lovely being here!

Kate Swann (8)
Rupert House School

I Wonder If . . .

I wonder if anything's under my bed?
Do you think I dare go and explore?
There's a shadow that's creeping up my wall
And a draught is moving my door!

I wonder if anything's in my wardrobe
Lurking amongst my clothes?
I'm hiding under my covers now
And shivering from my head to my toes!

I wonder if anything's behind the curtain?
It is swirling and floating around
Or maybe my window's wide open
And what is making that sound?

I wonder if anything's coming up the stairs?
I thought I heard one creak
I'm feeling very frightened
Do you think I dare go and peek?

Charlotte Martin (10)
Rupert House School

MY MEMORY

I have a memory
Of something I really hate
It's of a scorpion.

It lurked in the corner of my bedroom
And scuttled into my shoe
Its sting ready
For anything that moved!

I hated the way
It crept and darted
Its jet tail twitching.

Its black segmented body
Glistening in the moonlight
Its tail poised
The poison ready
To *strike!*

Tabitha Juster (9)
Rupert House School

CHOCOLATE!

Chocolate, chocolate, how I love it,
When I don't get any, how I crave it.
Chocolate, chocolate, it's the best,
Chocolate's better than the rest.

Chocolate is so good to eat,
Chocolate is the king of sweets.
Chocolate's yummy in my tummy,
'No more chocolate!' says my mummy.

Melissa King (9)
Rupert House School

THE GALLOPING BLACK HORSE

Smoothly he runs
Silently he slips by
A shimmer of black
Against the night sky

His inky tail tosses
In the starry moonlight
His black hooves they thunder
Through the endless night

On and on never ending
The shimmer of black
Gallops off to the west
With the devil on his back!

Jessica Moran (10)
Rupert House School

CART HORSES

I like to hear cart horses
They clip-clop on the road
I like the smell of their stable
And the way they pull their load.

I like the way they plod along
I like the way they look
I love to see them walking
On the road beside our brook.

Sophie Rothbarth (8)
Rupert House School

THE CAPTAIN OF THE SHIPWRECK

There's an old, battered shipwreck
Lying on the sea bed,
It's all black and broken
And all its crew are dead!

And if you look around
There's a wooden wheel house door,
And when you turn its handle
There's a skeleton on the floor!

It still wears a captain's hat
There's a hook upon his head!
There's a pistol by his hipbone
That is lying in the sand.

Eels swim through his eye holes
And his teeth are brown and rotten
He's the captain of the shipwreck
Which is lying on the bottom.

Alicia Holder (9)
Rupert House School

MY FIRST SNOW

I remember, I remember,
The first time I saw snow,
I looked out of the window,
And in the street lamp's glow.
I saw a million snowflakes,
Drifting softly down,
It was like a cloud had shattered,
And had fallen from the sky!

Daisy Lea (10)
Rupert House School

WILD HORSES

They gallop like the wind
They charge across the land
They go around in herds
And leave hoof prints in the sand.

They are so wild and free
They always run flat out
Their manes whip in the wind
They gallop and gallop about.

They buck and rear and kick
And fight and run at night
They graze all day long
It's such a lovely sight!

Charly Binney (9)
Rupert House School

MY SISTER

I remember when my sister was there,
She played with me all day,
And we had lots of laughs,
She didn't always have her way.

Now she has turned thirteen,
She's always having a kip,
She does nothing but eat chocolate,
And her bedroom is a tip!

Lucy Mace (11)
Rupert House School

The First Time I Ever Swam

The splash of water hit me,
It was a cool, comforting feeling,
I enjoyed wearing my armbands,
While holding my mum's wet hand,
I kicked and splashed till my legs ached,
My swimming costume stuck to my tummy,
We swam a bit more, I loved every moment,
And I went to the underwater land,
I was scared, very scared,
But I came up for breath all the same,
I was back in my mum's hands,
Safe and warm once again.

Alice Thornton (10)
Rupert House School

Memories Of Swimming With Dolphins

O dolphin curving through the wild sea,
Undulating your smooth tail,
Rising from the waters below,
Lateral fins steer and dorsal fins frail.

O dolphin gleaming in the sun,
Experts in surfing through the waves,
Sleek torpedoes slanting your fins,
Diving down to deep watery caves.

Elizabeth Sanders (11)
Rupert House School

MEMORIES OF THE SECOND WORLD WAR

I remember the battle cry,
As I marched into war,
The battle cries of the dying,
Who had gone before.

I remember the screams of men,
The screams of men in pain,
Of the dying on the battlefield,
Whom I'd never see again.

I remember the booming of bombs,
The wounded scattered the field,
The last cries of the doomed men,
Whose fate had already been sealed.

I remember the terror,
The terror of falling bombs,
Blitzing the nations defences,
Committing a million wrongs.

I remember the gun shots,
The speeding bullets of death,
Bringing anguish and horror,
Stopping the soldier's last breath.

I remember the bells,
Each funeral bell that tolled,
They rung throughout the country,
For the dead lying still and cold.

I remember the poppies,
The poppies so we won't forget,
The blood that was shed for our freedom,
To the fallen we owe such a debt.

Jessica Waddington (10)
Rupert House School

Muddy Paws

My cat and dog
Don't care
About the muddy paws everywhere
They just sit there
And stare!

Muddy paws
On the chair
Where you look they're everywhere
But they just
Don't care!

My cat and dog
Don't wipe their paws
The mud sticks to their grubby claws
And on the mat
They do not pause!

Stephanie Rigby (9)
Rupert House School

Fireworks

Scattering, fizzing all around
Fireworks flying in the air
People laughing everywhere
Children watching, screaming, crying, playing.
I see fireworks buzzing around in the sky
I see bonfires around
Burning flames in the sky.

Tabitha Jenkins (7)
St Andrews School, Wantage

SPARKLING, SPARKLING FIREWORKS

Sparkling, sparkling fireworks dancing, springing up and down
Whizzing round and round
Shooting fireworks, burning fire,
Blazing everywhere twisty fireworks, fizzing fireworks,
Look, bursting fireworks shooting in the sky,
Popping up so high
In the sky spitting as they go by.
Sometimes they are little,
Sometimes they are large,
But they are so wonderful
Let them go.

Rachel Spooner (7)
St Andrews School, Wantage

DOWN IN THE COAL MINE

In
The cage
It was dark
And a bell was ringing
I was squashed
It was cranked down and it was pitch-black
In the cage it was shaking and I was hot
And the cage was a box shape
And then there was a *bang!* And it was at the halfway
A couple of minutes later we were at the bottom of the coal mine.

Charlie Instone (8)
St Andrews School, Wantage

Down In The Coal Mine

First in the cage dark and scary
Bump
Ow!
That must be the halfway line
Boo! Who was that? Phew, it was only my friend
Bump
We must be there
First I was scared of the rumbling and shaking
But now I'm excited because we're there
Oh, I'm quite surprised
It's dark, scary and lonely
Arggh, it's a rat! Run for your life
Puff, pant, where am I?
Hey
I'm back where I started, back up the cage
Take off my hat, run back home
Mum, I'm all black
Go to bed, my dear, do what I say.

**Michael Garner (8)
St Andrews School, Wantage**

In The Dragon's Mouth

Slimy, slithery saliva
Really sharp teeth
Crunching and gobbling everything up
And down the tongue with meat.

Down the big hole swallowing food down
Yucky, stinky colours like dark red and brown
Swishing water down there
Oh, this is a very bad nightmare.

Looking at the bones going past the skull
Seeing all the jaws very, very well
Horrible black blood nearly everywhere
Yucky things around but I don't really care.

Georgia Phetmanh (7)
St Andrews School, Wantage

THE NIGHT SKY

Stars twinkling in the midnight sky
Brightly shining they wink at you
To you they look close but they are miles away
When you are gazing at them they will gaze at you
But stars, stars are a beautiful sight.

When the moon is lit
The stars awaken to find themselves
In the middle of the night
The moon with its pale face
Finds himself with company
And finds himself happy
Because stars are a beautiful sight.

Planets spinning round the stars
All colourful are they
They orbit round the stars and sun
Sometimes Jupiter or even Mars
Perhaps they have a moon of their own
But stars, stars, I love stars.

Jessica Murray (8)
St Andrews School, Wantage

THE CAGE

Dark, small box,
We all crammed in, squashed,
The doors slammed *shut,*
Ring, ring, ring,
Ready to go,
The cage shook, banged, bumped.
The chains rattled.
It jumped
And then carried on going down
Bumped
In the coal mine.

Ellie Wood (7)
St Andrews School, Wantage

THE WIND

The wind, the wind,
Blows, blows,
Around my head.
I like the wind
Going around my house.
God made the wind among the trees
Blowing around everywhere.
Don't know where, don't know when
Things fall down.

Nicholas Wood (9)
St Andrews School, Wantage

CATS

There was a man next door
(Who was rather poor)
Who had a cat
Which he rather wanted to scat.

There was a cat
Which had a funny head
And he spent all day
Wrecking the bed.

There was another cat
Which had a sore paw
And he spent all day
Licking it on the floor.

Rebecca White (8)
St Andrews School, Wantage

MY SCOOTER

For Christmas my dad gave me a scooter,
It was shiny and new.
I think it needs a hooter,
Because my bruises are blue.
I fell down potholes in the path
It really made me laugh.
I have found the brake, now it's too late,
My knees are sore, they are red raw.
I do like my scooter,
But please can I have a hooter?

Elizabeth Vickers (9)
St Andrews School, Wantage

THE GHOST CAR

Shadows on the trees,
Whistling, whistling.
What was that noise?
Swish, swish!
There it is again,
Oh, don't worry,
It is only the ghost car.

Brumm, brumm!
Stop, wait, listen.
Beep! Beep!
I'm scared,
Oh, don't worry,
It is only the ghost car.

Whoosh! Whoosh! Whoosh!
Ahhh!

Clare Gent (10)
St Andrews School, Wantage

THE STARS

I see them on a dark night
Those stars in the sky
Sparkling white.

The sky is dark blue
And you can see those stars
Looking down at you.

The stars are very far away
And when day has gone
They come out to play.

Dark is the night, bright are the stars
Around the other planets
Such as Jupiter and Mars.

Arabella Day (8)
St Andrews School, Wantage

MY ROBOT

My robot beeps and gloggs
He can play hide and seek.

He runs about and plays all day
But when it is time to go to bed

He shuts down and goes to sleep
Like me.

Then he gets up and starts all over again
And when I have to go to school

I leave him and he says 'Goodbye'
When I get back from school

We play and play until it's time for bed.
We go to sleep then until . . .
It's time to get up once again
And . . . we do the same again.

James Ballantyne (8)
St Andrews School, Wantage

My New Scooter

My new scooter has blue wheels
It's got a shiny, silver frame
And black handlebars
I love riding my scooter
I can go through puddles
I'm fast on my scooter down the hill
It has suspension
I have some safety devices
Which go with it
The first day I rode it
It was difficult
It's safe and reliable
I can fold it
I can stack it
I can pack it in a bag.

Toby Silverstone (9)
St Andrews School, Wantage

Stars

I always see the stars at night
Waltzing round the moon
I wonder why they dance
When no one plays a tune.

So silently the stars dance
With no music to follow,
While the moon up above
Smiles at them below.

But I think I know
The wise and clever man on the moon
Plays for the stars below
A quiet and special tune.

Serena Boheimer (10)
St Andrews School, Wantage

SWIMMING FUN

Go and get packed, get your swimming costume
Don't forget your hat.
Get in the car, look after your sister.
I'll get the money and the arm bands.

Here we are at the swimming pool.
You in your new costume looking cool.
Go in the changing rooms, there near the hall.
Hurry up; it's getting late.

Jump in the pool and have a spin.
Don't worry now, it's only a pool.
Let's go down the slide
No, let's go and hide.

Come on then, let's do both.
But look, they're playing golf.
Jump out now, they're closing.
If your feet are cold, rub your toes.

Look there's a pub, let's go and see it
Oh bother, I just stumped my toe
Let's go home now.
I'm tired now, but that was fun

Going swimming.

Olivia Palmer (10)
St Andrews School, Wantage

My Funny Robot

My robot is fun
He may seem a bit dumb
The only thing he wears is his metal suit
It makes him go toot, toot!

Left arm up, right arm down
Look, I can make him frown
He's friendly and strong
And he keeps on going ding-a-ding-dong.

My robot likes to bug me a sweet
Isn't that nice?
I love my robot so
Even when he twiddles his metal toe!

Kate Instone (9)
St Andrews School, Wantage

Kids

'Sit up straight,' said Mum to Mabel.
'Keep your elbows off the table.
Do not eat peas off a fork.
Your mouth is full. Don't try and talk.
Keep your mouth shut when you eat.
Keep still or you will fall off your seat.
If you want more, you will say please.
Don't fiddle with that piece of cheese.'
If, then, we kids cause such a fuss,
Why do you go on having us?

Eloise Jenkins (11)
St Andrews School, Wantage

My Robot

My robot ekes and cranks
The metal shakes about
My robot is big
He can lift me in the air
And when I go down the sofa back
He can lift the sofa and me.
When it's time to go to sleep
He tucks me in and clicks off
And goes to sleep.
We play in the morning
Games like football
But we broke a pane in the window
I like my robot
He is fun.

Alex Ballantyne (8)
St Andrews School, Wantage

The Sun

Every day coming,
Every day going,
Bringing a goldness,
Out of the black.

Every day climbing,
Over the heavens,
Sinking at sunset,
Soon to be back.

Coming and going,
Going and coming,
Leaving no footprint,
Leaving no track.

Vicki Coxon (9)
St Andrews School, Wantage

Planes

Some planes
Fly with people.
Some planes bomb
And blow up places.
And some planes
Take people on holiday.
Others just fly about
All day.
There are different planes
Made in different countries.
Some planes are faster than others
They use different airports.
Some planes are wider than others.
Planes show various colours
So we can see which country
They come from.

Thomas Smith (8)
St Andrews School, Wantage

My Robot

My robot is small
His name is Titch
He runs on the floor
And makes a noise.

You draw a line
On a piece
Of paper and
He will follow it
Round and round.

My robot likes to talk
And join in
My robot runs
Round and round
My robot is fun.

Thomas Masson (8)
St Andrews School, Wantage

FUN IN THE POOL

Me and my friend Charlotte
Have just been to the mall
We've got lots of bags of . . .
Cool toys for the pool.

Me and my friend Charlotte
Just got in the pool
We're playing with the cool toys
We brought for the swimming pool.

Me and my friend Charlotte
Just climbed out of the pool.
We had so much fun,
In the swimming pool.

Hannah Watts (10)
St Andrews School, Wantage

STARS

I wish I was a little star
You could see me from afar
I would twinkle in the night
See me shine, see me bright

I wish I was a shooting star
I would be faster than a car
Zooming across the midnight sky
People watching as I fly

I wish I was a lucky star
Wished upon from afar
Seeing people fast asleep
Making true their dreams to keep.

Charlotte Lewis-Pryde (8)
St Andrews School, Wantage

STARS

Stars that sparkle
Stars that twinkle
Stars that sparkle
All night long.

Stars are silver
Stars are gold
Stars are silver
In the sky.

Stars are shiny
Stars are bright
Stars are shiny
At midnight.

Hannah Stevenson (11)
St Andrews School, Wantage

FEAR

I am fear; I have lived since the Earth was made.
I was born in the light, but I turned away to the dark.
My sister is Hope, my greatest enemy.
I wear a black cape to cover my face -
So I cannot be seen.
Now I live in the centre of the Earth,
For I like to be left alone so I can do my job.
My greatest ambition is
To make everybody come over to my side
And leave Hope to wilt.
I have been around since the Earth was made
And I will be around forever.
I am fear and I will make your lives miserable.

Charlotte Drew (11)
St Edmund's RC Primary School, Abingdon

WINTER

I love winter, winter's great
Winter, great with snow on the ground
And we can go out to build snowmen
I love winter, winter's great
Ponds and lakes are frozen over
And I can go to ice-skate
Ducks try to paddle but skid and skate.

Aislinn Baird (9)
St Edmund's RC Primary School, Abingdon

A Journey

My family is in the car
We are travelling far.
We're catching a plane
And going to Spain.
We've sweets to pick
And my brother's been sick.
We're higher than birds
And feeling absurd.
We've come in to land
And the hotel is at hand
The end of a journey
To a hot land.

Hannah Brown (8)
St Edmund's RC Primary School, Abingdon

The Match

It was pouring down with rain
At the start of the game
I thought we were insane
Playing in the rain.
The goalie made a save
He thought he was very brave
It was a very close shave
Thanks to my mate Dave.

John Galvin (8)
St Edmund's RC Primary School, Abingdon

SEASIDE

We're on our way to the seaside,
We're gonna have so much fun.
We're going to the seaside
With everyone.

Have we got our fishing nets,
Have we got sun lotion?
Have we got all our pets?
Have we got a potion?

I like going fishing,
I like climbing too.
I like eating fish sticks
My brother kicks me too!

Sophie Bennett (8)
St Edmund's RC Primary School, Abingdon

JOURNEY AROUND THE WORLD

J ourneying around the world
O ver the mountains high and low
U nder the oceans deep and long
R iding camels over desert sands
N oisy polar bears on the icy snow
E gyptians building temples and tombs
Y ou, me and everyone must care for this planet.

Jack Dingwall (7)
St Edmund's RC Primary School, Abingdon

MY CAT

My cat is small and carnivorous,
With a house of her own.
I am jealous of the beauty that she owns.
She slaughters rats and mice,
With her long, shiny claws, sharp as knives.
She listens for a squeak or a scratch,
Never leaving her ground.
She hunts at night to kill a small morsel,
Fast as ever she catches it.
Her ancestors passed from Egyptian to Egyptian,
Twice as pretty.
The mystery of her is excitement,
Her luck has come and carried on past hate and love.
Her unusual eyes sparkle in the light,
She fascinates me like her ancestors
Fascinated the Egyptians.

Jessica FitzGerald (11)
St Edmund's RC Primary School, Abingdon

BIRTHDAYS

Birthdays are happy, birthdays are fun
Sometimes you might have a birthday bun.
The best part of birthdays is when Mum cuts the cake
After the birthday I can't stay awake.

Laura Molloy (8)
St Edmund's RC Primary School, Abingdon

EVACUATION

My wet sandals felt like a puddle of mud,
We all gathered up around the door of the carriage
Waving to our loved ones.
The train went off and all I could hear
Was the sound of terror and anger.
I went to sit down on the tatty chair
And I looked around to see who was there.
A man with no legs, a doll not quite finished
There was a loud noise outside
And a house burst into flames.
The train stopped and I felt a cold feeling
Inside my stomach.
Never before had I felt so lonely.
I soon found myself in a dark room
That smelt like bleach.
A lady as thin as a book called my name
And I felt like I was being auctioned.

Michaela Barklie (11)
St Edmund's RC Primary School, Abingdon

THE SEASIDE

The sea whistles,
The waves splash,
Dolphins jumping in a flash.
The people lay around all flat,
The wind has stolen Granny's hat!

Emily Pepperell (7)
St Edmund's RC Primary School, Abingdon

THE BAD DAY AT SCHOOL

I got up for school at the break of dawn
I set my alarm clock all wrong, it was only four in the morn.

I looked out the window to see what the weather was like
It was thundering and lightning, *oh no*, I had to ride my bike.

I got to school all cold and wet
'Where's your homework?' said the teacher,
Now Miss Meadows don't you fret.

'My homework is at home, I did it honestly Miss
But it got rather wet when my dog gave it a kiss.'

Things were getting worse when the lunch bell rang
I sat down to eat but in my sandwiches was ham.

As I finished my bread because I don't eat ham
I found myself confronted by the big bully Sam.

I ran away to hide but he saw me go
He pushed me to the ground because I was too slow.

He gave me a thump now I've got a sore head
I wish I was at home in bed!

I ran to tell Miss but she gave a big sigh
'Telling tales is for babies now don't you cry.'

The afternoon gets worse it's science for the rest of the day
My experiment's gone all wrong, my mixture is green instead of grey.

The teacher glared at me again, her eyebrows raised
I could see for sure that I wasn't about to get praised.

The bell just rang in the nick of time
My mixture just exploded and the walls are covered in slime.

I pushed my bike past the big bully Sam
He clenched his fists at me so I ran!

Now Mum's come in moaning all about the day she's had
And I thought to myself, 'Well maybe school is not so bad.'

Aislinn Campbell (9)
St Edmund's RC Primary School, Abingdon

MY BABY SISTER!

My baby sister was born
Hip, hip hooray
My baby sister was born
What a hectic day.
Her name is Ellie
Because she's got a big, round belly.
Her face is pink
And her nappies stink.
She cries all night
When you turn off the light.
She spits out her food
When she's in a bad mood.
If she gives you a lick
You're sure to be sick.
She'll squeeze your thumb
Then send a gas from her bum.
She goes to bed later than me
But even so I'm glad Ellie's a she.
My baby sister was born
Hip, hip hooray
My baby sister was born
What a hectic day.

Samantha Crossan (10)
St Edmund's RC Primary School, Abingdon

How Should I Feel?

The train seems to crawl noisily
And my parents are whimpering softly,
My heart is beating regularly,
The buildings are swaying cautiously,
How should I feel?

I'm not the only child on the train,
They are all crying unhappily,
I saw a policeman help patiently,
We all get off, a slow process,
How should I feel?

Many people are feeling low,
But how should I feel?

Stephanie Bennett (10)
St Edmund's RC Primary School, Abingdon

I Hate Spiders

I hate spiders!
Big ones -
Small ones -
Poisonous ones -
I hate them all!
They seem to be
Attracted to me,
I would not be surprised
If one is standing
Right behind me now.
Ahh! There is!

Charlotte Irwin (8)
St Edmund's RC Primary School, Abingdon

THE TYPICAL TROUBLES

The evacuees knew not of their fate,
Whether their parents were alive to appreciate,
Kindertransport and other plans,
To take their children from Hitler's hands.
Mrs Robinson, the teacher of the class,
Ordered the children to sit on the grass.
While they were waiting for the train,
Trying not to think of the terrible pain,
Going to the concentration camps they were told,
Yet all they could say was . . .
'Miss, we're freezing cold!'

Georgina St John (10)
St Edmund's RC Primary School, Abingdon

COLOURS

Red is the colour of roses
Blue is the colour of eyes
Yellow is the colour of lemons
Green is the colour of grapes
Orange is the colour of starfish
Pink is the colour of lipstick
Brown is the colour of leaves
Black is the colour of a cat
White is the colour of teeth
Grey is the colour of a pavement
Gold is the colour of a pen
Silver is the colour of money.

Kayleigh Pratt (8)
St Edmund's RC Primary School, Abingdon

TERRIBLE WEEK AT SCHOOL!

This is a poem about a school,
There was a boy who acted a fool,
His name was Ben, at least it was then,
Prepare for a tale of revenge.

On Monday morning, 9 o'clock,
Arriving late with the chickenpox,
People laughing and making fun,
He started crying and wanted his mum.

On Tuesday morning he arrived at school,
First lesson in the swimming pool,
Splash, splash, drip, drip,
He walked out casually
And then he tripped.

On Wednesday morning late again,
Driving the teachers all insane,
He made up with his friend named Wayne,
But that didn't last long because he was a pain.

On Thursday morning even later,
Straight to the headmaster, Mr Slater,
Walking slowly eventually arrived,
When he got in there he just sighed.

On Friday morning he arrived on time,
He made his way to the line,
With his books, pens and paper,
Straight to the headmaster, Mr Slater.

Kimberley Daly (11)
St Edmund's RC Primary School, Abingdon

EVACUATION

My mother, she waves goodbye,
As I go far away and cry.
The weather is cold and gloomy,
Rainy and wet, but yet,
I look forward to seeing my mum again.
My senses are haywire,
Whether to feel happy or sad,
But my mum will be waiting.
There are children around me swarming like bees,
The talking, mumbling, buzzing in my ears.
'It's alright,' people said but my feelings overwhelmed me.
The journey was long and tiring
And I fell asleep on the train.

Ruben Everett (11)
St Edmund's RC Primary School, Abingdon

TABBY CAT

Tabby the cat has fur like silk,
Teeth like razors ready to bite.

Pads like sponges, eyes like lights,
Shine and shimmer in the dark night.

His tail is like a balancing stick,
Always ready to make a quick switch.

Like thunder his purr so loud,
He waltzes around looking ever so proud.

Emily Tooher (10)
St Mary's School, Henley-on-Thames

DREAMS

I have a dream
Where there are no cars or trains
I have a dream
Where there are no fights or guns
I have a dream
Where animals aren't killed for food
I have a dream
Where trees aren't cut down for wood
I have a dream
Where everyone lives in peace
I have a dream
Where no one suffers.

Purdey Miles (10)
St Mary's School, Henley-on-Thames

CAMEL

A tongue-twister
A moaner-groaner
A desert-walker
A water-carrier
A grumpy-hump
A wide-eyed
A spitting-mammal
A lazy-lump.
A beat-beat

James Burke (10) & Krysha Shahi (9)
St Mary's School, Henley-on-Thames

RATTLESNAKE

Dangerous needles, ready to inject
Pointed fangs like sharp icicles.

Sensitive listener, waiting for something
Every move is silent . . .

The slithery body like a wet tube
The sleekest mover, never seen.

Camouflaged killer ready to bite
A bullet shot from hell like death!

His rattle is like a maraca.
    Rattle, rattle
        Squeeze
            Gulp!

Amy Biart (11) & Matthew Welfare (10)
St Mary's School, Henley-on-Thames

SHARK

Grey and white like a winter's sky
A massive beast, so cunning, so swift
The tail, a powerful motor
Propels it through the water
The fin, slicing through the waves
Skin like sandpaper
Eyes like black holes
Teeth like razors
Rows and rows like people in a queue
The smile, the last you'll ever see.
Snap!

Christopher Jeanes & Hannah Dodds (11)
St Mary's School, Henley-on-Thames

EAGLE

Soaring on a pale blue sky.

A speck above the golden trees,
Its talons streamlined, pointed daggers.

Pinpointing eyes, seeking out prey
His bulleting body, pelting downwards.

Silhouetted against a darkening horizon,
The cruel, black outline like a ripple on water.

His sunset feathers ruffling like willows,
Gliding over the rolling hills.

Wings like the swish of the breeze.

Celeste Harber & Elliott Butler (10)
St Mary's School, Henley-on-Thames

A CAT KENNING

A fat ball
A toe tickler
A mouse eater
A dangerous dropper
A cautious stroller
A food finder
A longing purrer
A wall walker
A night cat-a-waller
A tail swisher
A fast mover
A quick gobbler
A milk slapper.

Emily Atkinson (10)
St Mary's School, Henley-on-Thames

DREAMS

When I dream,
I go into a world,
With nobody there but me,
I can swim with blue whales
And talk to all creatures,
There are no cars or guns,
There are no roads or paths,
The sun never dies,
So there is no sunset or sunrise,
There are no wasps or hornets,
Just friendly bees,
The animals aren't kept behind bars or in houses
They just run wild and free,
There is no evil just good,
There is life but there is also death.

Lauren Fisher (10)
St Mary's School, Henley-on-Thames

DREAMS

A dream is like a soft breeze,
Smoothly spreading in your mind
A dream is like a wisp of memories rushing back
A dream is like a fortune teller, showing the future
A dream is like a final destiny, getting nearer
A dream is like a gentle myth, telling the story
A dream is like a jarred secret, enlarging around you
A dream is like a warm happiness getting colder.

Isobel Dodds (9)
St Mary's School, Henley-on-Thames

DREAMS

I dream of taking pictures
from all around the world,
of lions casting shadows on Africa's blood-red sky,
dolphins rolling the weaving waves,
like horses galloping through a field of seas.

I dream of taking pictures
of birds skimming a scarlet sky,
a remembered image of glimpses from the past,
a panther pounding through oceans of grass.

I dream of taking pictures
to record the beauty of the world
and safe forever locked away,
in a place I dream of every day.

I dream of taking pictures
and keeping them all my life.
A remembered thought,
safe forever.

Alex Barker (11)
St Mary's School, Henley-on-Thames

ROBIN HOOD

Robert of Locksley
is heroic Robin Hood
fighting with laser-sharp arrows
fiercely battering people he doesn't trust
wanting revenge on the sheriff of Nottingham
Robin is fantastically clever in every way,
when Robin fights he always wins.

Emily Jones (9)
Uffington Primary School

ROBIN HOOD

R espectful and merciful man
O thers he thinks of day and night
B rave and courageous with his bow and arrow
I n many ways a natural leader of the Merry Men
N ever gives up, always tries again

H unter of deer, creeps through the forest
O beys the king, waiting for his return
O utlaw - that's Robin the leader of the gang
D resses in Lincoln green, that's all he's got.

J J Keene (8)
Uffington Primary School

ROBIN HOOD

R obert
O f Locksley
B rave, fearless outlaw
I n Sherwood Forest
N ew outlaw and wolf's head

H e is
O ut and about
O utcasts hunted by the sheriff
D etermined to kill the Locksley outlaw.

Andrew Baxter (9)
Uffington Primary School

ROBIN HOOD

The bravest outlaw in the land
Lives in the forest
Rides a horse
A camouflaged poacher
Wears Lincoln green to hide in the forest
His quiver has
Sharp, killing arrows
The traveller coming by
Will get a surprise
For Robin Hood steals from the rich
To give to the poor.

James Allen (10)
Uffington Primary School

ROBIN HOOD

Robin
Hood is
the toughest
hunter in Sherwood
Forest. His arrows are
razor sharp. His bows are
strong. Robin camouflages
himself in the woods.
Hiding from enemies
who want to kill
him but they
won't kill
him.

Peter Jones (9)
Uffington Primary School

ROBIN HOOD

R obin Hood
O utlaw
B ow and arrows hanging on his back
I n the forest, creeping about
N ever giving up

H iding from the sheriff's men
O ccasionally creeping round the forest
O n the look out for the sheriff's men
D etermined not to give up.

Mark Hagreen (9)
Uffington Primary School

ROBIN HOOD

Robin Hood is one of the few good,
His enemies bad,
His friends good,
An excellent bowman
Never misses his target,
His arrows fly swiftly,
Swifter than anyone's in the land,
Sherwood Forest is his home
And his loyal friends too,
Second to none and proud to be the one.

Peter Long (10)
Uffington Primary School

CONNECTICUT

Soaring miles above the ground,
breaking free,
as free as a bird,
up above the clouds,
travelling to a faraway land,
coming into paradise.
Suddenly,
you're a rushing ant,
under immense stress,
to finish the job,
fighting to keep your strength up,
enough strength to keep you going.
Suddenly,
you're a mouse among cats,
dodging, swerving,
trying to get through the blockade,
to the safety of your mouse hole,
to get a rest,
to relax.
Suddenly,
you're a sloth,
slow,
pacing,
no worries to do anything,
to accomplish anything.
Suddenly,
you're a ravenous crocodile,
chomping,
slashing,
devouring your prey.
Suddenly you're breaking free.

Chris Keene (10)
Uffington Primary School

ROBIN HOOD

A fearless fighter,
a legendary bowman,
slau ghters his prey with one deadly arrow,
when it comes to a fierce battle, victory is always his,
victory is the outcasts,
danger is unknown to this man
and always will be because,
he is the greatest of the great,
best of the best,
a legend in history,
he is Robin Hood.

Ollie Baily & Angus de Wilton (9)
Uffington Primary School

ROBIN OF LOCKSLEY

Sneaking down the wall
crouching from the soldiers
wearing a feathered hat
climbing on the wall
solid brick wall
deadly arrows on his back
sword in the scabbard
looking for the money.

Matthew Young (9)
Uffington Primary School

ROBIN HOOD

T he sheriff of Nottingham's adversary
H iding in the
E vergreen forest

L iving with the outcasts
E xiled
G reat leader
E veryone his friend
N ow his battle for justice
D etermined to stop the sheriff

O f Nottingham
F rom his massacre

R eign of terror
O btaining cash for the impoverished
B ut the unstoppable sheriff wants to finish it
I t's impossible
N ever, ever loses

H oping to influence the sheriff to cease
O utrageous, outstanding
O utlaw
D emanding peace.

Jason Haynes (8)
Uffington Primary School

THE LEGEND

The legendary Robin Hood,
Fearless at heart,
Heroically avoiding sheriff's men,
Commander of outlaws,
Training his band
To split willow wands at six hundred paces.

Guilt encircles his father's life,
Determined to have his revenge,
To bring King Richard, the Lionheart home,
Excitement is his only drawback,
At times putting himself and others in peril,
Hunting to survive,
Owning nothing from the sheriff.

Hallucinating his unavoidable death,
Poison ends his eventful life,
Buried under Sherwood earth,
Where the arrow lay.

The legend of Robin Hood,
Lives on.

Tom de Wilton (11)
Uffington Primary School

Robin Hood

R obin Hood
O utrageous outlaw
B orn to fight and see justice done
I n his world
N ever gives up, it's his duty

H ooded, secret, devoted man
O utcasts' leader, brave and fearless
O utwitting the sheriff of Nottingham
D oing his duty for the poor.

Peter Wren (8)
Uffington Primary School

Robin Hood

The bravest outlaw in the forest
Shooting deer far away,
Wearing Lincoln green
Camouflaged amongst the trees and bushes,
Green stranger on horseback.
Laughs in the face of danger
A strong poacher covered in mud.

Alex Gaffka (8)
Uffington Primary School

ROBIN HOOD

Robert of Locksley
The one and only
Robin Hood
Adventurous fighter
The outcast of the forest
Never gives in
A hooded, secret stranger
He's a law breaker
A gifted bowman
Steals from the rich
Gives to the poor
An impressive swordsman
Kind at heart
Cannot be immobilised
A respectful man.

Peter Osmond (9)
Uffington Primary School